Contemporary Design in Detail

Sustainable Environments

Yenna Chan

BEVERLY MASSACHUSETTS

ROCKPORT PUBLISHERS

First published in the United States of America by
Rockport Publishers, a member of
Quayside Publishing Group
100 Cummings Center
Suite 406-L
Beverly, MA 01915-6101
Telephone: (978) 282-9590
Fax: (978) 283-2742
www.rockpub.com

Library of Congress Cataloging-in-Publication Data available

ISBN 13: 978-1-59253-230-8
ISBN 10: 1-59253-230-6

Series Editor and Art Director: Alicia Kennedy

Designer: Chris Grimley for over,under

Cover image: Single Speed Design, Big Dig House
Photograph by Single Speed Image

Printed in China

Sustainable
Environments

Contents

Introduction   8

Response to Place   **14**
Site Specificity   16
Site Conservation   36

Connection to Habitat   **56**
Bioregionalism   58
Environmental Interface   76

Conservation of Resources   **100**
Alternative Energy Sources   102
Hydrological Systems   122

Use of Building Materials   **140**
Elemental and Experimental Materials   142
Salvaged and Recycled Materials   166

Directory of Architects and Designers   186
Photographer Credits   190
Acknowledgments   191
About the Author   192

Sean Godsell Architects, Future Shack

Introduction

The film *Powers of Ten*, by designers Charles and Ray Eames, begins with a view of a man napping on a picnic blanket in lakefront Chicago, then zooms out to a point in the universe ten million light-years away, and back in again to reveal a single proton contained within the man's hand—a shift in the scale of things that forges a connection between the minutest object and the world at large. Sustainable design suggests a similar relationship. Contrary to so much of architecture—especially residential, whose mandate stops at the property line—sustainable building recognizes that the social, economic, and environmental effects of each detail lie far beyond the bounds of the object.

Sustainable architecture is a broad categorization, with no single formal, spatial, or theoretical typology. A wide spectrum of design philosophies may be included, from the scientific, which strives for self-sufficiency in zero-energy systems, to the poetic, which seeks to create meaningful spatial contexts for experiencing nature. Their commonality resides in the ethical intent of sustainable design's twofold objective: the well-being of the inhabitant and the conservation of the environment. Even then, the notion of intent may become murky when sustainability occurs as a byproduct of design. Consider how the act of reuse derived from *aesthetic* or *theoretical* decisions drives many projects today that reincorporate into buildings the cast-off components of an industrialized society.

Once seen as being outside of the design mainstream, sustainable architecture is now the fastest growing segment of the industry. More and more, sustainable monographs urge us to rethink how products are designed and manufactured.[1] Practices such as prefabrication and modular assembly promote affordability—a social facet of sustainability often overshadowed by the environmental benefits. New materials and technologies based on renewable resources offer improved building performance in the areas of safety, durability, and material strength. Competitions at every level, from local to international, have captured public interest and generated momentum toward making sustainability the norm. Since many of these competitions result in commissioned buildings, they not only encourage designers to adopt environmentally conscious practices, but also serve as testing grounds for the cooperative efforts of the construction trade, designers, and clients in realizing innovative ideas.[2]

Increased public awareness of environmental problems (both present and anticipated), coinciding with a movement away from formalist theories in architecture, has created advantageous conditions for sustainable design. Founding thinkers in the effort to build sustainably focused on processes rather than questions of representation, but their ideas about mass production, thermal mass, and ecological communities have prepared the way for contemporary projects with similar ideals that take advantage of newer technologies and methodologies. In these new works, formal and conceptual principles are often integrated with environmental technology to produce truly avant-garde designs. Yet quite as often, these projects do not require complex advancements in building science to present original, contextual solutions.

This volume examines recent architectural investigations into sustainability in the context of residential environments—urban, suburban, and rural—around the globe. Rather than present the work of these leading and emerging practitioners project by project, we have organized the material according to the strategies by which they have explored sustainability through design. These categories form a progression from the broader conceptual concerns of siting to the immediacy and tactility of materials.[3] The first two sections, "Response to Place" and "Connection to Habitat," include projects that focus on architecture's relation to the physical context, whether by reducing the design's impact on vegetation

Shim-Sutcliffe Architects, Island House

and species or by modulating the climate through the building envelope. The third and fourth sections, "Conservation of Resources" and "Use of Building Materials," collect projects that minimize the drain on our environmental capital and introduce affordable, ecological materials into their design. All the works recognize the interconnectedness of these issues. Most combine more than one aspect of sustainability, and although we may have singled out a specific detail, it is not because it characterizes the project entirely, but because it represents a particularly effective or innovative demonstration of the strategy under consideration.

The details in this volume show that architects are able to create environmentally mindful structures while maintaining rigorous design inquiries into the usual matters of form, space, and dwelling. Together, the projects selected for this book raise fundamental questions about the impact of environmental concerns on the design process and the relationship between sustainability and architectural form. Despite the diversity of their projects, these architects approach sustainable elements as far more than items on a checklist for design—a methodology reinforced by the LEED system of points. Textbook methodologies of sustainable design typically look at active technologies, such as solar or wind-generated power, and passive technologies, such as thermal mass, through the lens of building science. But as the canopy of photovoltaic panels in Pugh + Scarpa's Solar Umbrella House demonstrates, sustainable technologies can also inform architectural expression.

We have chosen to explore sustainability within the framework of the residential environment to uncover the factors affecting the fundamental aspirations of responsible design. Sustainable living appeals to people at the most concrete level of their lives, bearing on common concerns of health, comfort, and utility, while invoking altruism. Sustainability has become a form of populism, and despite skepticism about the effectiveness of grassroots efforts, proponents believe that small changes made at the individual, domestic level will eventually reach critical mass.

Although alternative technologies often necessitate a high set-up cost, limiting their accessibility to higher economic levels,[4] cost-conscious passive design has always played a significant role in vernacular buildings—a strategy largely ignored in today's cookie-cutter developments. Working at the small, manageable scale of a residence lets designers experiment with new sustainable methodologies, which may preclude the "greenwash" sometimes incurred with high-profile commercial or institutional clients and legislated standards in larger typologies.

The design industry has discovered that sustainable living environments may be the most direct way to reach the public. In January 2005 *Dwell* magazine selected Escher GuneWardena's elegant proposal to construct as its Dwell Home II, which took as its program "Building Green."[5] Endeavors such as this serve as models for architecturally and ecologically progressive homes produced within realistic parameters. These projects often involve partnerships with developers, government organizations, and sponsorships from manufacturers. Although residential construction remains dominated by non-architect-designed, unsustainable buildings built for profit, this type of media-driven interest in sustainability has the potential to shift consumer demand. It might even allow architects to regain some of the market in residential design.

One final note: Architects are well aware of the incongruities in making a single-family residence environmentally friendly. The single-family house allows for too much land usage per person,[6] strains the distribution of resources, potentially takes up arable land in rural areas, and is often sited away from public transportation. Since it is an enduring typology in architectural practice around the world and unlikely to disappear in the near future, we have included a large but diverse number of strategies that address current ideas of sustainable design at this scale. Fortunately, architects have begun to incorporate sustainable elements into high-density urban dwellings. Designs such as Balmori Associates' vegetated roof on the Solaire Building in Manhattan, which alleviates problems of pollution, lack of porous drainage surfaces, and the urban heat island effect, provide more than a rare encounter with nature in the city.

Above all, the details of sustainable residences presented here remind us that a well-designed building, whether green or brown, is not an assortment of technological requirements but a network of associations, whose effects assume a meaning to the inhabitants and their community far beyond the material and mathematical.

Notes

1. *Refabricating Architecture: How Manufacturing Methodologies Are Poised to Transform Building Construction* by Kieran Timberlake Associates and *Cradle to Cradle: Remaking the Way We Make Things* by Bill McDonough and Michael Braungart come easily to mind.

2. The C2C Home International Design Competition and the Emerging Green Builders' Natural Talent Design Competition are but two examples.

3. There are equally significant sustainable practices affecting residential communities at the regional level, such as land-use planning, infrastructure, and economic programs. While many excellent projects rely primarily on such practices, these topics exceed our scope and thus could not be represented here.

4. Europe has seen many efforts to make multiunit housing developments sustainable. In New York City, the Earth Pledge Green Roofs Initiative is sponsoring a number of green roof conversion projects that involve affordable housing groups.

5. Also in 2005—in one indication of the mainstreaming of sustainability—*Sunset*, a magazine devoted to suburban life in the West, presented to the public its decidedly less modern Green-Built Idea House, developed with California's Sustainable Building Taskforce and the builder Clarum Homes. Earlier that year, however, the magazine collaborated with Michelle Kaufmann to showcase the eco-oriented modern prefab home, the Sunset Breezehouse.

6. Not only does the house occupy a large area, but more, its residents occupy a large ecological footprint: "Calculations show that the planet has available 1.9 hectares [4.7 acres] of biologically productive land per person to supply resources and absorb wastes—yet the average person on Earth already uses 2.3 hectares [5.7 acres] worth. These 'ecological footprints' range from the 9.7 hectares [24 acres] claimed by the average American to the 0.47 hectares [.11 acres] used by the average Mozambican" ("The State of Consumption Today," Worldwatch Institute, 4 February 2004).

Escher GuneWardena, Dwell Home II

Response to Place

Each of the houses in "Response to Place" draws on the topographical and surface characteristics of the land as a starting point for its design. The focus here is the way the buildings connect to the ground, whether built into the earth, as exemplified by many projects in "Site Specificity," or resting lightly above it, as seen in "Site Conservation." In reality, these divisions are not constructed from the building's relationship to the ground plane, since the Slavin-Arnholz and the Oxford Gardens Residences would fall into the opposite group from which they are now placed. The two groupings derive, rather, from the different philosophical objectives of blending into, and becoming part of, the landscape or preventing changes to ecological and topographical conditions throughout the building site.

The landscape—considered here broadly as topography, vegetation, or even the surrounding view—is a strong determinant in the design of the houses in "Site Specificity." It may, for example, lead to the use of a certain building profile or material. In every case, the structure and form of the house adapts to the conditions of the site, asserting that each condition warrants a unique solution. These works address the visual impact of buildings on the landscape, yet it is not merely an architectural response to the landscape that their designers elicit. By refusing to impose on its site, each of these houses aspires to facilitate in the inhabitants a deeper understanding of, and greater connection to, their environment.

The houses are set into agrarian, wilderness, and suburban contexts, and although the two suburban projects inhabit sloped sites the outcomes could not be more different. Of these projects, the Island House is perhaps the most wholly integrated into its environment. Not only do its green roofs, planted with native vegetation, allow it to blend in visually, but its harvested groundcover enables it to participate in the local agricultural economy. With the Reeve and Slavin-Arnholz Residences, the existing trees provide a reference point for the houses' relationship to their sites. Both create a response through the use of sympathetic materials—wood in the first case, copper in the second. The Reeve house develops an architectural articulation of the weathered tree line; the Slavin-Arnholz, one based on the verticality of the tree trunks on the sloping lot. By disappearing into the treescape, moreover, the Slavin-Arnholz addition never overpowers the older original home in front, even though it almost doubles the living space. For its part, the Sloping North House adapts to an undesirable plot of land in a new development by turning the problematic condition of its steep slope into an organizing principle for the residence that links inside with outside.

"Site conservation" seems an odd term to use when talking about the construction of a building, since the process involves disturbing both existing ecosystems and natural grading. How does a building conserve a site, when, by its very nature, it occupies a footprint on the land? The architects of the residences presented here address this dilemma in a twofold manner: First, they find the least damaging way to erect the house, minimizing excavation and eliminating tree removal; second, their designs impact the existing site very little once constructed. More than a generalized respect for the land, their strategies show ways of adapting architecturally to maintain ecological habitats for flora and fauna and existing topographical patterns affecting site drainage. The Kropach/Catlow Farmhouse, for example, required the slightest regrading. Raised off the ground on post foundations, both the Åland Summer House and the Price Residence ensure that the roots of nearby trees remain undamaged. The Price Residence, in particular, considering its breadth on the upper levels, reduces its actual contact points with the ground to a surprisingly bare minimum.

Using land that has already been developed, rather than unbuilt or agricultural land, is always preferable, as exemplified by the Gulf Island, Wheatsheaf, and Oxford Gardens Residences. The latter two works introduce yet another consideration of conservation, since it is hardly the primeval forest (rapidly disappearing and not an option in most parts of the world) that they are conserving. The Wheatsheaf house considers the potential of one form of developed land, a former tree plantation, as an environment that is gradually regaining a natural balance. An odd corollary to conserving this landscape is that the building also guards against the site's natural hazards. For Oxford Gardens, conservation means building downward to replace one green space with another on the same urban site. It maintains public open space by cleaving to strict zoning requirements, and it provides a new habitat for local birds in the process.

Although not illustrated here, of great interest to the design community of late are brownfields: unused sites that contain some form of contamination, often, but not always, once occupied by heavy industry. Site remediation techniques tend to be expensive, which, together with the larger size of many brownfields, makes their development more common for mixed-use complexes or communities. The BedZED project, examined later in "Alternative Energy Sources," is rebuilt on reclaimed land that required environmental study. Thus, the conservation of a site is just the first step in an approach to design that is often termed "minimal impact." This idea encompasses strategies throughout design, building, and occupancy to reduce the effects of architecture on the land, from the house footprint to altered site conditions, from the use of site resources to the production of waste.

rooted, harmonious, integration, locus, sheltered, natural palette, terrain, agrarian landscape

Site Specificity

Shim Sutcliffe Architects, Island House, Thousand Islands, Ontario, Canada

The house is situated on one of the Thousand Islands, home still to a number of dairy farms. To preserve the agrarian nature of the surroundings, the 5-acre (2-hectare) meadow around the house was hydroseeded with a regional clover mix, which a neighboring farmer harvests a few times yearly. The house presents a more private face to the road, while, on the other side, it opens onto expansive views of the St. Lawrence River.

Above and Right The house and its garden spaces constitute a variety of landscaped surfaces. These include two levels of green roofs, covering 1,700 square feet (157.9 square meters), that connect to the natural site through plantings, texture, and color. The upper green roof is planted with indigenous wildflowers. A dry garden and a green court are both sheltered by the 200-foot (61-meter) concrete retaining wall that is cut into the low incline of the site.

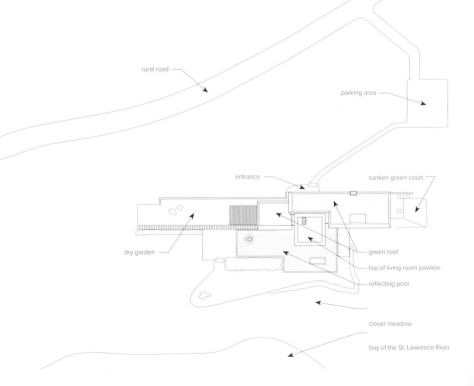

Above Four varieties of sedum (*S. album, S. floriferum Weihenstephaner Gold, S. kamtschaticum ellacombianum,* and *S. spectabile Brilliant*) are cultivated on the lower green roof. The roof plantings reflect the colors of the clover meadow below, while the gravel of the eaves repeats that of the dry garden.

Above Where the house faces the river, full-height glazing in the kitchen, dining, and living spaces takes in a sweeping panorama of the landscape. The reflecting pool in the foreground wraps around three sides of the living room pavilion; the water garden contains native water lilies and bulrushes.

Right The green roof is integrated into a built-up roof with a modified bitumen membrane over wood and steel-frame construction. The 5-inch (127-millimeter) soil mixture rests on top of a geotextile filter cloth, an expanded polystyrene drainage board, and the membrane roof. The thin profile of the eaves, visible in most of the photographs, is achieved by the soffit extension beyond the green roof that stops at the building envelope.

Opposite Four ground surfaces come together at the corner of the reflecting pool: Their planarity complements the level landscape of the surrounding farmland and creates a balanced man-made landscape in harmony with the natural one.

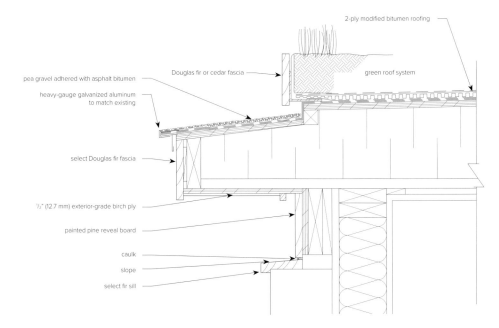

**Cutler Anderson Architects,
Reeve Residence, Lopez Island,
Washington, United States**

Positioned at the edge of the woods of Lopez
Island on the northern end of Puget Sound,
the house responds to the steep topography
of the coastal zone, which changes from
woodlands to rocky bluffs to floodplain
before reaching the ocean. The green roof,
with its 250 tons (226.8 metric tons) of sod,
follows the downward slope of the land and
reflects the hues of the coastal plain. The
monopitch vegetated roof creates a minimal
disruption to the site, and the architecture
choreographs for the inhabitants a meaningful experience of living within the landscape.

Above The two sides of the house reflect the different conditions of the inlet seascape and coniferous forest. The design expresses a close relationship to the land through architectural form and construction and finish materials. Elements such as the tall wood columns, natural wood shingle siding, and bluestone terrace help to establish an emotional response to the site.

Left The sketch elevation reveals how the low-pitched roof follows the angle of the wind shear of the surrounding trees. This both shields the house from strong winds off the sound and blends the building into the landscape.

Above The rough stone wall and bluestone plinth anchor the building into the stone cliffs; although the double-face veneer wall is rectilinear and even, its connection to the cliff appears virtually seamless.

Right Nestled into the woods, the house is reached by two footpaths from the main roadway and parking area. Visitors are rewarded with dramatic vistas as the paths arrive at openings between the wings of the building. The tripartite plan allows for both views and access between the sides of the house, while creating an arrangement of spaces suited to family living.

Opposite Built-up timber columns with steel connectors attaching to the roof and stone base are found on both sides of the house to support the green roof. The forest façade, finished in natural red cedar, presents a more subdued character.

**Sambuichi Architects,
Sloping North House, Yamaguchi, Japan**

The house reconsiders the value of leftover or undesirable land, drawing from it a rich living experience integrated with the site. Building the home on an extra tract of land on a north-facing slope in a new housing estate saved the owner a considerable sum; however, the contextual and natural aspects of the site were valuable, as the surrounding area is naturally wooded, with views of the Seto Inland Sea to the east and the Chugoku mountains to the north.

Above The roof slope of 11:18 was determined by the incline of the natural terrain and the architectural requirements of maintaining adequate light, ventilation, and heat. The structure of the house is concrete, partly underground with a raised roof plane that allows light in along the four sides and through a roof window. The building solves the perceived negative siting condition by working with the landscape and environment rather than against it. Forgoing high-tech products and relying on natural conditioning methods kept the project economical as well.

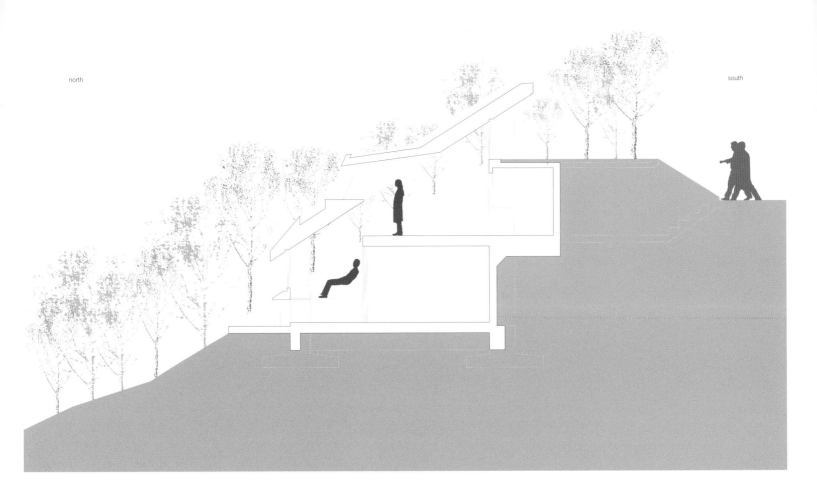

Above The house was built for a family of four, with private spaces on the lower levels progressing to the common spaces on the upper level. This organization reflects the character of the site, with the more open and distant views at the top of the slope. Living areas are located toward the edge of the slope with utilities in back.

Opposite An opening in the center of the north incline defines the small dining area and alleviates the severity of the steep pitch. The roof seems to float above the floor due to the continuous band of glass around the four sides of the home and the near identical finish of the floor and ceiling planes. From within the house, the lack of floor-to-ceiling glazing never interferes with the sense of the environment outside. The open interior is divided only in a few places, with full-height glass partitions, to maintain the flow of space, light, and air.

Above Two interior levels in the house allow for views into the woods and above the tree canopy. Although the house is excavated into the hillside, the roof window allows for a feeling of being in the treetops, as it frames the view to the mountains. The wood finish of the ceiling wraps around the sides of the opening to create a continuous surface.

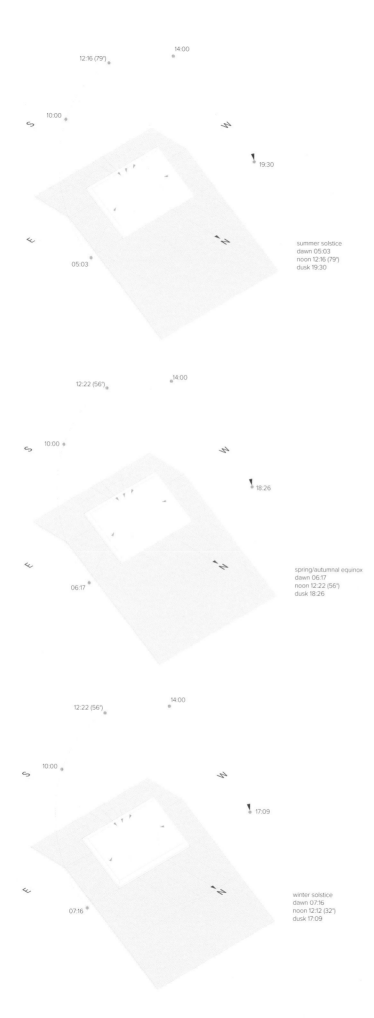

12:16 (79°) 14:00

10:00

S W

19:30

E

N

05:03

summer solstice
dawn 05:03
noon 12:16 (79°)
dusk 19:30

12:22 (56°) 14:00

10:00

S W

18:26

E

N

06:17

spring/autumnal equinox
dawn 06:17
noon 12:22 (56°)
dusk 18:26

12:22 (56°) 14:00

10:00

S W

17:09

E

N

07:16

winter solstice
dawn 07:16
noon 12:12 (32°)
dusk 17:09

Left During the summer, the raised concrete form shelters the interior from the sun, and the open plan circulates cool air from the bottom of the slope to the top. The slope allows the low winter sun to enter, however, and creates the feeling of a winter garden. A constant climate can be maintained in the space throughout the seasons due to the modest amount of exterior wall in contact with fluctuating air temperatures outside.

**Travis Price Architects,
Slavin-Arnholz Residence,
Washington D.C., United States**

The design is a four-level addition to the back of an older home on a steep and narrow site on Rock Creek Park. The layered, multiple decks that terrace down the slope provide the owners with much-needed outdoor living space and play areas, since the steep topography barred a usable rear yard. The house celebrates the tall, upright forms of the existing treescape. By using a column structure with pinpoint footings for the addition, all major trees on the property were retained. Trees even integrate with the structure, growing through openings in the lower decks.

Above The structure approximates the verticality of the tree trunks on the site without mimicry of form. Shade from the foliage helps to lower the cooling loads for the house, a significant reduction for this warm, humid climate. The design also promotes the natural admission of light and air through a consideration of the sun angles and cross ventilation. In addition, a green roof system helps to keep rainwater runoff to the nearby stream and park at a minimum.

Above Abundant glazing at the house and frameless glass guardrails on the decks reflect the foliage and sky, producing an impression of lightness as the architecture is sublimated into the landscape. The copper and steel finishes of the exterior harmonize with the natural palette of greens.

Right The addition more than doubled the space of an early twentieth-century Tudor-style cottage. From the street, only a small portion of the stair tower is visible above the slate roof of the existing house and barely so due to the dense foliage. Thus, the addition preserves the small-scale feel of the street. Saving an existing house and its infrastructure is a significant strategy in introducing sustainability to established neighborhoods: Here, it allowed the owners to stay within the city limits rather than moving to a more distant suburb and avoided the wasteful tear-down syndrome of "monster" houses replacing smaller ones on urban lots.

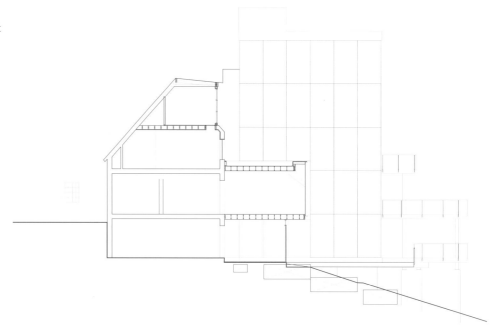

Above Every opening celebrates the changing light and vistas through the wooded site. A reveal at the ceiling and floor hides the frame and sill of the window to achieve a sense of continuous verticality in the view, which reinforces the forms of the trees directly outside. The glass is highly insulated and argon filled.

raised structure, preservation, land use, minimal impact, footprint, existing infrastructure

Site Conservation

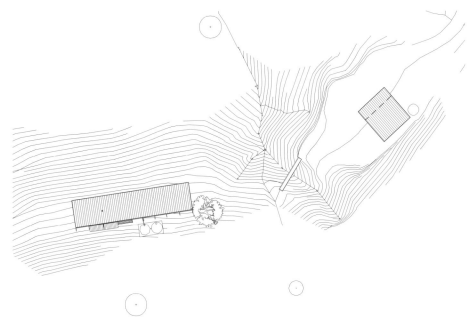

Grose Bradley Architects, Kropach/Catlow Farmhouse, Myocum, Australia

The house is located in a verdant farming valley on gently sloping terrain. Positioned on an east-west axis with views of Mount Warning to the north, the linear plan grants comparable vistas to all family members. The building site does not disrupt the surrounding countryside: Other than a low fence, few visible markers inscribe the property onto the land.

Above Right The repeated elements of the steel frame allowed for efficiency and economy in construction. The ground was excavated only at each pier for the structure's foundation and footing, which minimized soil erosion during the building phase.

Right A deck on the western side of the house provides sheltered outdoor space. Adjustable broad-bladed louvers on the end façade keep it cool, obviating the need for complex mechanical systems that would disrupt the environment from an auditory or visual standpoint.

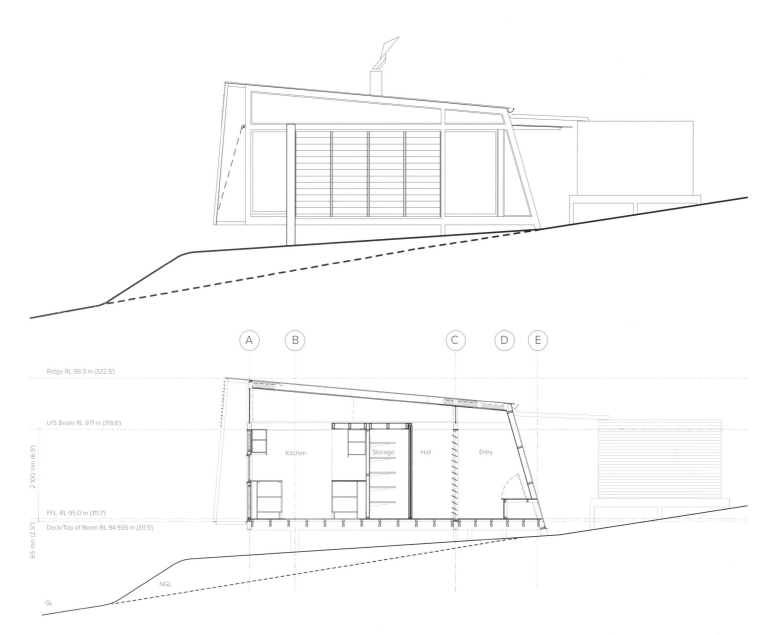

Ridge RL 98.3 m (322.5')

U/S Beam RL 97.1 m (318.6')

2 100 mm (6.9')

Kitchen   Storage   Hall   Entry

FFL. RL 95.0 m (311.7')

65 mm (2.5')

Deck/Top of Beam RL 94.935 m (311.5')

NGL

GL

A   B   C   D   E

Above As seen in the west elevation and north-south building section, the elevated platform allows the descending ground plane to slide beneath it—a low incline that is reflected above in the corrugated metal roof that opens the house up to the expansive landscape. The design called for minimal filling and grading of the site.

Saunders & Wilhelmsen Arkitektur, Summer House, Åland, Finland

This summer residence is erected on post foundations so that the ground and tree roots below would remain undisturbed, allowing the building to be sited near existing trees. Raising the structure slightly minimized the need to regrade and restore the surrounding earth, which was particularly effective since the site and region is quite flat. As a result, the house could be located close to the ground without steps up to the platform. This proximity to grade provides a sense of intimacy with nature for the inhabitants; the roof terrace (whose access stairs are visible on the right) offers better views of the nearby islands. Building on posts also facilitates the reading of the structure as a continuous folding plane that rests lightly on the land. In fact, the architects describe the cabin as an architectural landscape that transforms itself from wall to floor to roof.

Above Construction materials were kept simple and natural, including woven linseed fiber insulation and cold-pressed linseed oil finish for the pine exterior walls. All of the wood, including the interior birch plywood finish, was obtained from a local sawmill.

Travis Price Architects, Price Residence, Washington D.C., United States

The street façade of the architect's residence is an abstract patinaed copper curve that hangs from two 18-inch (457-millimeter)-diameter, 66-foot (20.1-meter)-high red columns anchored by steel cables at the edge of a cliff. The tree trunk that seems a part of the house's structure hints at efforts to keep changes to the site at a minimum. A section of the wall cuts inward to accommodate the tree, which is framed by a glazed vertical slot. Although the front of the house appears broad, the building in fact approaches the ground with a small square base where the heavy columns sit on 10-foot (3.1-meter)-deep post foundations.

Above Left A view through the treetops reveals multiple suspension points for the structure and the cupola on the open roof terrace. Throughout the house, the unique structural system is left exposed and painted a consistent red. The proximity of the large oak and birch trees is also evident—the design saved all the large trees on the site.

Left The property backs onto the Rock Creek Park area where a stream bed feeds the creek that leads to the region's major waterway. Because the project required significant environmental and planning review, the design minimally affects the soil and trees, and the building is literally suspended above the ground by the cantilevered system. The house contacts the ground at a few points only: the large columns, the 40-foot (12.2-meter)-long anchor in front, and a vertical support for the deck at the back. The rest of the building cantilevers off this system using solid suspension rods, cantilevered steel-tube beams, and counterweights.

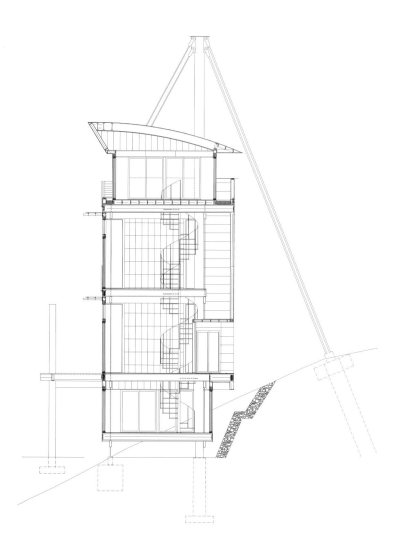

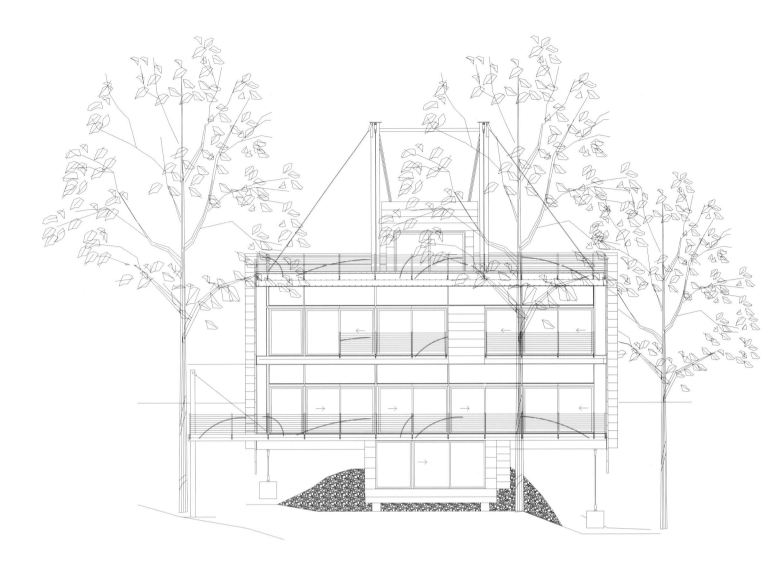

Above The building is wide, relative to its narrow section. This balancing act is clear in the rear elevation, which reveals the similarity of the structure to a suspension bridge. The large expanse of insulated storefront glazing brings the outdoors inside.

Opposite The counterweights are steel tubs that weigh 5 tons (4.5 metric tons) each and serve to stabilize the building against hurricane-force winds hitting the back wall. Beyond the weight, a notch is visible in the curved deck that wraps around a tree trunk, almost in line with the tree on the front façade. The design circumvents the problems of building a large footprint along an uneven and steep terrain that is complicated by the combination of disturbed fill and underlying bedrock.

**Battersby Howat Architects,
Gulf Island Residence,
Mayne Island, British Columbia, Canada**

This retirement residence is built on previously cleared land, replacing a smaller cottage. A trace of the previous house is found in the new concrete walls on the north and east sides, which maintain the footprint's old boundaries. The new structure extends over a rise in the land toward the west, fitting in between large existing trees on the north and south sides. Again, no trees were felled. To obtain more floor space, the house is cantilevered beyond the concrete foundation on the southern, glazed façade.

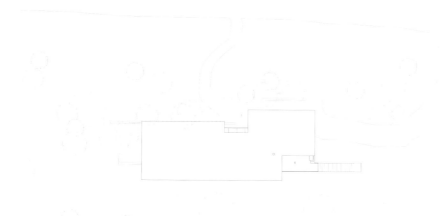

Left The new design also conserves the existing infrastructure of the older cottage; the pedestrian and vehicular access to the house, the septic field, and well were all retained. Rebuilding on the same footprint required planning permission because of the residence's proximity to the waterfront and road. To reposition the house, however, would have meant clearing additional land, including many large trees, and relocating the utilities and services—more detrimental disruptions, overall.

Jesse Judd Architects,
Wheatsheaf Residence, Wheatsheaf,
New South Wales, Australia

The forest that encircles the house is a former
state logging plantation, last seeded with
eucalyptus thirty to forty years ago. Although
the residence is situated not within an old-
growth forest but within vegetation with a
monocultural growth and little underbrush,
its elemental expression still bears in mind
its environment, which is slowly reverting
to wilderness. Even as the house minimally
impacts the wildlife habitat into which it is
set, it takes protective measures against the
natural conditions. Of primary concern are
bushfires; evidence of past fires is visible on
the trunks of the messmate trees. Thus the
metal-frame building, whose factory-finished
steel shell is noncombustible, sits on a platform raised above the ground on posts, and
is surrounded by gravel.

Above The design takes certain cues from the vernacular of structures of the Australian bush—such as the simple form of corrugated metal opening onto a wood verandah—yet it clearly defies expectations of organic integration into the landscape with its black exterior and glowing red interior. The metal roof aids in collecting rainwater that is filtered for drinking, toilet tanks, and irrigation and channeled to two large water tanks at the rear of the house.

Above The platform is raised only to the extent that code does not require a handrail, and only at the bedroom end of the house does it step down to grade. The deck, made of reclaimed turpentine wood from the old Woolloomooloo Wharf in Sydney, creates a safe area for play and rest away from snakes and other creatures of the bush, but allows the wildlife to roam freely or find shelter beneath the house.

Right The lightweight metal-frame construction enables the house to hover above the ground with a minimal foundation structure. At its thickest point, the structure is 180 millimeters (7 inches). The underside could thus be made fire resistant, with few protrusions for utilities. The smooth, discrete metal form also references the nomadic character of portable vehicles and holiday homes.

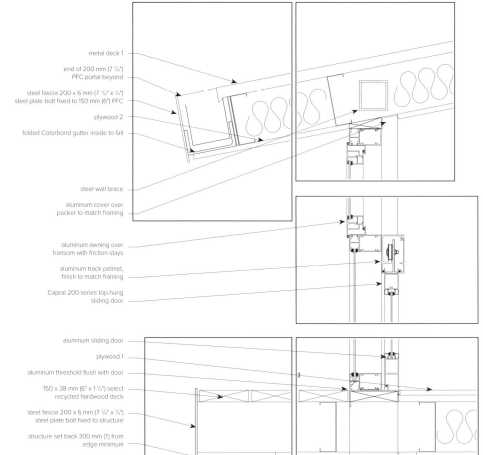

metal deck 1

end of 200 mm (7 ⁷/₈") PFC portal beyond

steel fascia 200 x 6 mm (7 ⁷/₈" x ¹/₄") steel plate bolt fixed to 150 mm (6") PFC

plywood 2

folded Colorbond gutter inside to fall

steel wall brace

aluminum cover over packer to match framing

aluminum awning over transom with friction stays

aluminum track pelmet, finish to match framing

Capral 200 series top-hung sliding door

aluminum sliding door

plywood 1

aluminum threshold flush with door

150 x 38 mm (6" x 1 ¹/₂") select recycled hardwood deck

steel fascia 200 x 6 mm (7 ⁷/₈" x ¹/₄") steel plate bolt fixed to structure

structure set back 300 mm (1') from edge minimum

Above The interior finish on walls and floors consists of sustainably sourced hoop pine plywood, a native timber. As the tree canopy is very high, the house has no spectacular views. Consequently, the residence is more internally focused; in the architect's words, "womblike."

**Michaelis Boyd Associates,
Oxford Gardens Residence,
London, United Kingdom**

This family residence preserves the expanse
of a designated open lot and adheres to the
stringent North Kensington neighborhood
planning regulations by building underground. The house rises no higher than 1.8
meters (6 feet) from street grade. A curv-
ing ramp descends from the street to the
entrance, between concrete retaining walls
that host abundant plantings. The vegetated
roof of the house, satisfying both environmental and planning board needs, is planted
with sedum, wild strawberries, and thyme.
As the surface has become part of the local
ecosystem, other flowers have self-seeded.
Replacing the original green space with a
new vegetated roof has in fact improved
what was a derelict urban lot littered with
junked appliances.

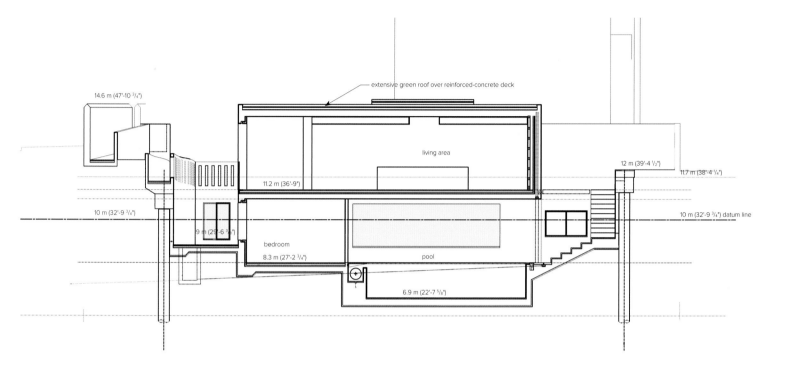

extensive green roof over reinforced-concrete deck

14.6 m (47'-10 ³/₄")

living area

12 m (39'-4 ½")

11.7 m (38'-4 ¼")

11.2 m (36'-9")

10 m (32'-9 ³/₄")

10 m (32'-9 ³/₄") datum line

9 m (29'-6 ³/₈")

bedroom

pool

8.3 m (27'-2 ³/₄")

6.9 m (22'-7 ⁵/₈")

Above The site was excavated to a depth of 4 meters (13.1 feet) for the cast-in-place concrete structure. The structural requirements of building underground called for the use of concrete, but it also provides thermal mass, preventing extreme fluctuations in the interior temperature. Along the sides of the building, solar panels have been added to increase the efficiency of the building systems; photovoltaic panels to generate electricity; and thermal panels for the domestic hot-water system.

Above and Opposite Although its external form is somewhat austere, the interior dispels any myths about underground living: The spaces are airy and well illuminated by a skylight and large windows. The first level is open to the pool on the lower level (also accessible by a slide made of Corian). Similar to a geothermal heating system, the water in the home is obtained without cost from an aquifer 100 meters (328 feet) underground—a well was drilled in the yard. Once processed through a heat pump, it is used for hot water, radiant heating, and in the pool. The pool also functions as a heat sink, keeping the temperature throughout the house constant.

Connection to Habitat

The design strategies found in "Connection to Habitat" address sustainability through an architectural correlation with a regional definition of place. The determination of a regional condition is geographic but broadly scaled, whether drawn from solar angles at a particular latitude, local meteorological conditions, or a specific architectural vernacular. In each case, the habitat maintains a close relationship with its external environment by adapting to and learning from its locality. The differences between various climactic and cultural contexts is not emphasized here so much as the variety of the methods attuned to regional conditions, since these residences are, in fact, all located in the northern and southern temperate zones.

Bioregionalism carries a broader implication beyond architectural practices. Often it refers to the cultural and political economy of a specific geographical location and applies to large-scale issues of dwelling, including the social and economic. A bioregional approach to sustainable residential design considers local origin as fundamental to its architectural methodologies, played out especially in the types of construction materials used and the source of these materials. Of critical importance is the building's involvement with the local economy—through labor, production, and consumption. At its simplest, it can be understood as using environmentally harvested wood grown on native soil and purchased at a local lumberyard, thus minimizing pollution from transport and stimulating the local building trades.

The four projects gathered under "Bioregionalism," however, more specifically demonstrate the influence of the vernacular in contemporary design. Each integrates traditional architectural details, building practices, and materials in ways that ground the home in a particular place, yet respond to the needs of inhabitants of the twenty-first century. And each projects adds to the experiential and connotative, the environmental dimension. The Split and Black Houses and the Kropach/Catlow Farmhouse make use, respectively, of earthen walls, cement fiber, and corrugated metal enclosures as common, locally available materials that draw on local building traditions. The layout of the Split House shows clearly how this adaptation can unfold from regional housing typologies. The Black House and the Water Villa, as outgrowths of the building typologies of the barn and the houseboat, are unmistakably contextual. Architecturally responsive to the conditions of their agrarian and marine landscapes, these homes nonetheless possess identities quite distinct from other interpretations of their types, as they avoid any literal rendition. Such work vehemently opposes the interpretation of the vernacular on a purely representational level (found in so many tract houses in Europe and North America) as a stylistic application that ignores the climactic and material basis of the original forms.

The projects in "Environmental Interface" explore habitat through the boundary between exterior and interior climates. For these houses, the designers articulate the building envelopes—insulated and fenestrated wall types, surfaces with thermal mass, solar chimneys, and green roofs—to take advantage of natural means of heating, cooling, and ventilation. Often underused in mainstream building, passive technologies are design based and virtually free, making them a low-cost, efficient way to condition interior space through simple physical principles. The Great Bay and Gulf Island Residences and A House for the Future incorporate largely glazed south-facing façades and more protected northern elevations to introduce light and solar gain in winter while keeping out the cold. All three projects feature passive solar design through shading devices, building orientation, and solar radiation, A House for the Future is a purer demonstration of traditional passive solar techniques, with its massive walls and stone floors that reradiate heat, while the Great Bay Residence exemplifies the solar-tempered house that uses solar gain as heat but does not store it.

The last two decades have seen the establishment of performance standards based on passive technologies, leading to designs that feature superinsulated exterior envelopes, reduced energy consumption, and efficient ventilation and water conservation. Many, like A House for the Future, rely on passive solar principles to eliminate a typical furnace or boiler system. More experimental and unusual systems, such as the glass solar stack wall at the Little Tesseract House, and the porous rock base of the Stone House, base their innovations on traditional principles of ventilating and circulating air through a building using convection. These homes require an open layout that encourages the circulation of air upward and siting that takes advantage of prevailing breezes. Of course, mechanized systems within the building envelope are now available for ventilation and shading. These active façades employ photosensors to control environmental conditions in larger multiple-dwelling buildings where manually operated shades and fenestration are not always expedient and solar exposures not always flexible. Nevertheless, as will be seen in the ecovillages of the section "Conservation of Resources," passive methods remain a significant factor in creating energy efficiency, even where used in conjunction with active ones.

Projects that feature vegetated roofs have been distributed throughout the book according to the diverse objectives of this enclosure system, including A House for the Future, whose green roof appears in "Hydrological Systems". In each case, the vegetated surface contributes to a stable thermal environment within the building. A particularly compelling iteration, examined here, belongs to the green roofs of the Solaire Building, a sustainable residential high-rise in Manhattan. By absorbing or deflecting solar radiation, rather than reflecting it back into the densely populated environment, Solaire's two large vegetated roofs lessen the urban heat island effect. Additionally, during photosynthesis, the vegetation absorbs carbon dioxide and releases oxygen, which helps to alleviate the greenhouse effect. Increasingly, in cities around the globe, architects are imagining the beneficial effects that would accrue if even a fraction of the roofs were green. Among the many single-family houses considered here, the Solaire Building stands out further as an example of how habitat comes into play in an urban environment.

Often using low technological means, the projects of "Environmental Interface" immerse their inhabitants in the natural environmental conditions in which they live. As Hiroshi Sambuichi, the architect of the Stone House, would say, these methods are a way of "picturing the Earth's details through architecture."

vernacular language, contextualism, local economy, building traditions, regional typologies

Bioregionalism

**Mole Architects, Black House,
Prickwillow, Cambridgeshire,
United Kingdom**

The Black House adopts the regional language of barn structures in an iconic and thoroughly contemporary manner. Located adjacent to a farm field, the house borrows its materials and proportions from the corrugated cement-fiber barns that dot the flat landscape—the sole local building vernacular, as the Fens region was only reclaimed for farmland in the prior two-and-a-half centuries. The factory-finished black cladding covers the walls and roof of the tall, rectilinear three-story home, whose form is in keeping with the gabled profiles of the boxy brick houses in the village.

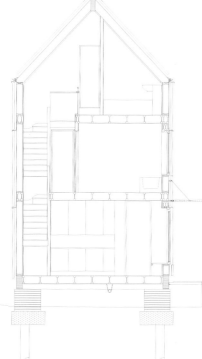

Left The structure consists of prefabricated timber panels insulated with recycled newsprint and engineered wall studs from wood byproducts, resulting in a relatively trim 200-millimeter (8-inch) thick wall. The structure of the house is supported by a glulam beam ring on concrete piers faced with brick, one of the typical local materials. The piers, in turn, rest on pile foundations. The elevated base of the building facilitates ventilation of the structure, which again follows the typology of local farm buildings that were built up on brick piers to keep out the wetland dampness.

Opposite and Above Left The precision of the detailing—such as the alignment of the cladding with the window heads and the use of contrasting zinc flashing—refines the simple, industrial material and offsets the deep corrugations of the cladding. Brise-soleils above the ground-floor windows on the west façade help shade the interior from the summer sun. Other environmental measures include insulated glazing with an argon gas fill and a low-e coating, as well as reduced fenestration on the north façade. A heat pump provides the heat for water and a forced-air system.

Architectuurstudio Herman Hertzberger, Water Villa, Middelburg, Netherlands

The Water Villa is a natural progression of houseboat living, ubiquitous to the waterways of Dutch cities. Many such residences now seem closer to floating buildings than to boats, and even include multiple dwelling units. Unlike a boat, with its cramped quarters and poor thermal qualities, the Water Villa is a proper house, generously glazed, with a living room and kitchen above and bedrooms and bath at water level. The multiple terraces, the low-maintenance steel shell, and the hold (consisting of the floatation tube), however, link the structure to a maritime typology. The villa presents an alternative to the problematic development of land: Excessive reclamation has meant that much of the land near the North Sea coast is below sea level and in constant threat of flooding—a threat of increasing concern with global warming.

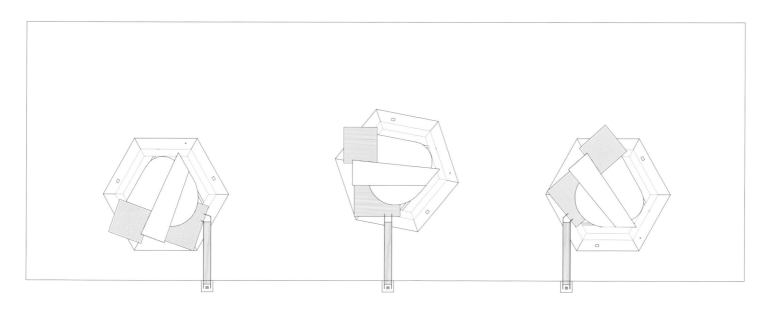

Above The floating structure allows the inhabitants to adjust its orientation for solar gain or shading—or simply to vary the view. Operated manually or by computer, the villa can revolve almost 90 degrees about the point of the gangway attachment. The design may be modified to accept a vegetated roof for further energy efficiency, and an optional floating garden may be added adjacent to the villa.

Opposite The architects studied industrial building systems and materials, such as those used in shipping and transport. The process led them to produce a lightweight structure consisting of a steel frame covered by a light steel façade and with steel-plate concrete floors. The interior is made of insulated steel compartments, but it also incorporates a more tactile wood finish, with plywood walls and wood door and window frames. Because the structure is partially prefabricated, with major components brought to the site and assembled there, the villa can be built in a short period of four months.

Above An 8-meter (26.2-foot)-long gangway provides access to the villa from the concrete pier on shore. It is attached at the villa by a pivot point to allow for the rotation of the structure but anchors it securely to prevent drifting. Winch cables run from the shore at two points, attaching to the structure at several locations to keep the villa steady during rotation or high winds. Since the house is considered to be a permanent structure attached to the shore, mortgages on the property are allowed.

**Atelier Feichang Jianzhu,
Split House, Yanqing, Beijing, China**

Set in a mountainous region near the Great
Wall, the house introduces several layers of
sustainability through adaptations to context
and siting. The parti of the house is based on
the traditional Beijing courtyard home, but is
transformed through its angled layout, which
opens on one side to the mountains. Moreover, a natural stream meanders through the
site under the house, creating a *shan shui si
ye yuan*, a courtyard house with mountain
and water.

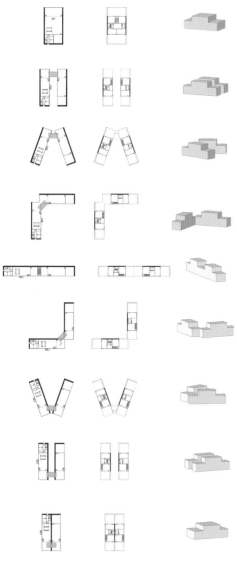

Above Rammed-earth walls line the exterior faces and free ends of the split bars; elsewhere, wood siding emphasizes the striations of the rammed earth. The earth walls are insulative and can be sourced and fabricated on site, providing an ecological and cost-effective alternative. The organic material also allows the walls to biodegrade naturally at the end of their use, becoming once more a part of the landscape.

Above and Right The split form preserves the site's existing trees, whose greenery enhances the more dramatic landscape beyond. The plan organizes the house into public and private zones and allows for only one wing to be used when fewer residents occupy the home, thus saving energy.

Above and Left The construction materials follow the long-established practice in China of *mu tu*, or earth and wood buildings. Inside, the structure of the house consists of laminated wood. The wood elements of fenestration, staircase, and exposed framing give the interior a warmth and tactility that contrasts with the stone floors that seem to be a continuation of the mountainous terrain outside.

Above The design was developed as a proto-type for several other homes to be built in the vicinity. The plan adjusts to the hilly topography in the valley neighborhood by altering the angle between the two wings to create a number of different configurations, from parallel wings to an inversion of this form.

Grose Bradley Architects, Kropach/Catlow Farmhouse, Myocum, Australia

The residence employs the vernacular language of an Australian farm building, the lean-to shed, creating a spare and practical design for the sunny, arid climate. The farm shed's utilitarian materials—steel-frame structure, corrugated-metal shed roof—are combined with simple shading devices and a straightforward layout to open up the house to the environment but provide shelter from the elements. Fixed anodized aluminum sunscreens at the top of the steel frame run along the length of the house and are lowered at the kitchen bays to shade its horizontal band of windows. Rainwater is collected (another common practice in this climate) and channeled directly from the gutter at the lower end of the shed roof into a corrugated metal storage tank behind the home.

Right The house's metal frame is fitted with operable glass louvers adjacent to the fixed glass planes to control ventilation. Exterior roller shades installed at all the large glazed bays double as insect screens. These shades move along guides to fasten at the base of the steel armature protruding beyond the north façade. A total of three different forms of louvered surfaces, from transparent to opaque, are incorporated throughout the house for cross ventilation and shading.

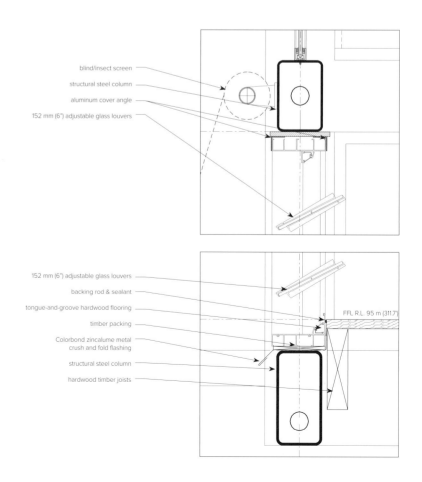

blind/insect screen

structural steel column

aluminum cover angle

152 mm (6") adjustable glass louvers

152 mm (6") adjustable glass louvers

backing rod & sealant

tongue-and-groove hardwood flooring

timber packing

Colorbond zincalume metal crush and fold flashing

structural steel column

hardwood timber joists

FFL R.L. 95 m (311.7')

Above The living space resembles a pavilion, yet the glass barely registers as the focus is not on the large amounts of glazing but the continuity of the outdoors, inside. The deck at the west end of the house appears as an extension of the interior. With sliding glass doors, louvers, and roller shades, the inhabitants have multiple options for shading and ventilating. In another climate, to locate shading devices on the north elevation would be unusual, but here, the prevalence of sunny days and the wide solar angle in summer put the shades to good use.

Above The south side of the building is well shaded with the roof overhang and solid walls faced with corrugated steel. There is less glazing on this elevation, but light is admitted through clerestory windows and a low window along the hallway floor, allowing the sun to illuminate surfaces rather than heat the space. The raised walkway with a metal grating contributes to the sense of agrarian utility and semipermanence.

Opposite Partitions are kept below the level of the clerestory to encourage the transmission of air and light, but where necessary, clear glazed panels extend to the roof to provide privacy between rooms. One section of the hallway features adjustable aluminum louvers to further control solar radiation while letting in light.

bioclimactic, thermal mass, vegetated surfaces, passive ventilation, insulation, photosynthesis

Environmental Interface

**Steven Holl Architects
in collaboration with Solange Fabiao,
Little Tesseract House,
Upstate New York, United States**

The house brings together spatial and functional experiments: It examines the prototype of a solar stack wall for nonmechanical climate conditioning within a warped form that interprets the fourth-dimensional understanding of a cube. The dark stucco cube with extruded steel windows adds dining, sleeping, and studio spaces to an older building, from which it obtains its basic power and utilities. The cube connects to the existing stone house by an exoskeletal steel frame, a space that functions as a dining porch and contains the stair to the second-floor studio.

Right The glass stack wall is oriented toward the south to take advantage of winter solar gain. The existing building is actually quite low and therefore does not block the angle of the sun. North winds are deflected by the prowlike edge of the opposite side of the house. In addition, roof-mounted photovoltaic cells back up the system during power outages.

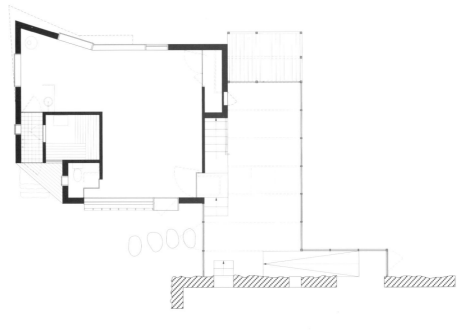

Above Pivoting windows and doors open the L-shaped dining porch to the outdoors during the summer to admit light and ventilation to the addition. In winter, a Danish wood stove helps heat this cooler space. The porch also mediates the two sections—distinct in form and material—of the home.

Above The interior of the residence is very open, particularly the second floor, and the solar stack wall is visible through the house. Made of German structural channel glass, the stack wall represents the firm's initial application of the material for heating and cooling. The hollow plenum, used for passive solar gain in winter and cooling via the stack effect in summer, spans two stories on the exterior and becomes translucent fenestration for the rooms inside.

Above Left Flaps at the base and top of the glass channels control air intake. During the winter, they are closed so that the sun warms the air within—and thus the interior—through radiation. Even without warm air ducted to the second floor, the interior temperature is often 50 degrees warmer than the winter air outside. Top and bottom flaps are opened during the summer so that the exterior air circulates up through the wall in the manner of a solar chimney. The frog pond immediately below helps cool the air that is drawn in at the base of the glass wall.

Pill Maharam Architects, Great Bay Residence, Newmarket, New Hampshire, United States

Unlike a true passive solar house, this residence is solar-tempered: Sunlight heats the structure but is not stored. The tempered house contains less thermal mass but must balance a number of functions (insulation, air tightness, heat recovery) to achieve energy efficiency. The south façade has argon-filled low-e aluminum-clad windows for passive solar heat gain and a high roof overhang for shading. Large glulam beams supporting the roof create an open plan in the interior, which allows the southern sun to warm the entire space. Operable clerestory windows exhaust the hot air.

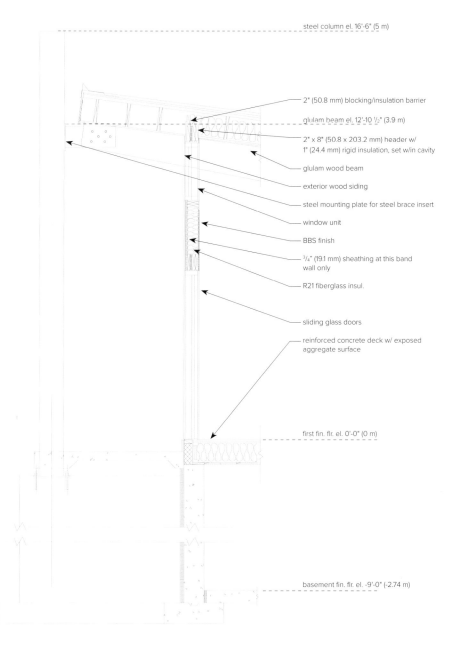

steel column el. 16'-6" (5 m)

2" (50.8 mm) blocking/insulation barrier

glulam beam el. 12'-10 ½" (3.9 m)

2" x 8" (50.8 x 203.2 mm) header w/
1" (24.4 mm) rigid insulation, set w/in cavity

glulam wood beam

exterior wood siding

steel mounting plate for steel brace insert

window unit

BBS finish

¾" (19.1 mm) sheathing at this band
wall only

R21 fiberglass insul.

sliding glass doors

reinforced concrete deck w/ exposed
aggregate surface

first fin. flr. el. 0'-0" (0 m)

basement fin. flr. el. -9'-0" (-2.74 m)

Above Left As in a passive system, the building orientation is critical. Set on a ridge on an east-west axis, the house consists of two bars that bend toward the southwest along natural topographical contours to follow the sun's path. The solar features are combined with a geothermal heating system that circulates well water through the house, using a heat pump to bring the water to the appropriate interior temperature. Even the air conditioning (seldom used due to the natural cooling) is run from the geothermal system. The water also provides hydronic radiant heating. With all environmental features considered, including renewable finishes, the house earned a five-star Energy Star rating.

Left The amount of sunlight to be admitted through the southern window during the fall and spring determined the depth of the roof overhang. Even as the overhang provides shade in summer and light in winter, its details may be finessed to allow specific amounts of solar gain during the temperate seasons. The glulam beams are supported by posts let into metal brackets. Durable metal is incorporated elsewhere as vertical siding and standing seam steel roofing. The low-slope metal roof is appropriate in the cool climate of New Hampshire as well as in warmer regions. Like the walls, it is highly insulated.

**Battersby Howat Architects,
Gulf Island Residence,
Mayne Island, British Columbia, Canada**

Function and aestheics come together in a
house whose strong formal expression meets
with environmental efficiency. A wide stretch
of storefront glass (with argon fill and low-e
coating) allows for passive solar gain but also
maintains ample light levels in the overcast
West Coast climate. A pair of cantilevered
forms—3 feet (.91 meters) each at the first
floor and roof overhang—shades the level
below. The aluminum storefront and the zinc
roof were chosen for their low maintenance
and stability in the coastal climate.

Above Fewer openings on the north and east elevations guard against heat loss and provide a measure of privacy from the road and neighboring homes. The wood rain-screen cladding appears in sheltered areas of the house to create a more human scale and texture at the entries.

Above and Right The standing seam roofing wraps down around the prefabricated roof trusses and the vertical wall on the north in a protective gesture. The vertical window and skylight above it represent the only fenestration along this façade, illuminating the dining area and stairwell to the ground floor, where there are additional bedrooms, storage, and a garage. This zone also articulates the gap between the house's old footprint and the new.

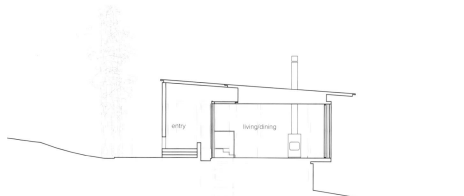

entry   living/dining

Above During the summer, the foliage just outside the south face tempers the sunlight in the interior with changing shadows and reflections. The open plan—the entire first-floor program, including bedroom and bath, is doorless—encourages circulation of air throughout. Finishes are kept simple and the construction technologies conventional, reflecting the local economies of labor and suppliers.

**Jestico + Whiles, A House for the Future,
St. Fagans, Cardiff, Wales,
United Kingdom**

Passive technologies and context-appropriate construction methods have resulted in a house that produces almost zero carbon dioxide emissions. To store solar radiation, the architects combined greenhouselike glazing on the south side with heavy earthen walls (finished with an oak rainscreen and lime render), built with bricks made from clay excavated on site. A heat pump generates ambient heating. The absence of gas service to the area encouraged the use of renewably sourced electricity from a plant; however, photovoltaic cells mounted to the roof alleviate the utility expenditure. Native materials, such as the oak post-and-beam frame insulated with sheep's wool, reduce embodied energy arising from transport.

Above and Left The south side of the house contains open living spaces on the ground floor, while the north side and upper level hold the more private, enclosed rooms. Motorized blinds shade the roof light in the living room when required. The design incorporates cross ventilation through operable windows and passive ventilation ducts, and the moderate climate allowed the architects to use air infiltration for introducing fresh air. Radiant floor heating relies on ground heat from below the frost line, 1 meter (3.3 feet) below grade, transferred to liquid in tubing that circulates from yard to house.

Sambuichi Architects,
Stone House, Shimane Prefecture, Japan

The architect considered this project as an equation that balances energy use, from the manufacture of materials to the operation of the building. The design takes advantage of the natural properties of simple materials to create climate-appropriate conditioned space. In this mountainous region of ski resorts, the climate is one of extremes: Heavy snow and north winds during the winter contrast with high heat and humidity during the summer. Additionally, because rice fields surround the house, the land is quite wet during the growing season. The structure consists of a ground-floor residence used year round and a three-season guest annex, buried in a crushed stone base as a passive ventilation strategy. The stone mediates the interior and exterior conditions, adjusting the effects of humidity and temperature.

Opposite The enclosed but unconditioned garden and court face south and occupy the front portion of the house. Air enters at this lower end, cooling as it passes through the rocks to circulate within the house and out through the terrace at the top and opposite end of the house. The terrace, facing north, serves multiple functions: as a solarium in winter, a space for drying laundry during the rainy season, and a shaded terrace for entertaining in summer.

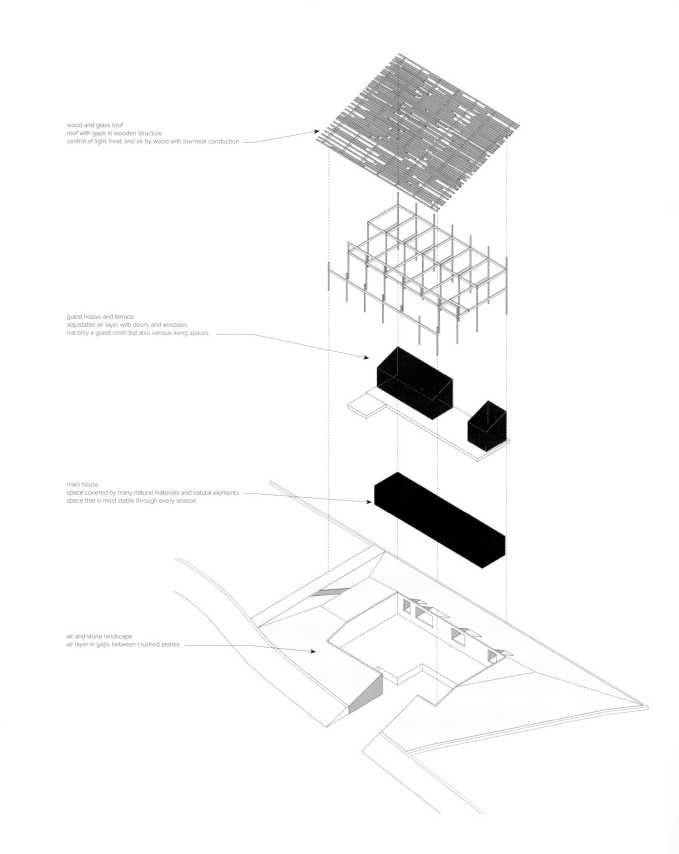

wood and glass roof
roof with gaps in wooden structure
control of light, heat, and air by wood with low-heat conduction

guest house and terrace
adjustable air layer with doors and windows
not only a guest room but also various living spaces

main house
space covered by many natural materials and natural elements
space that is most stable through every season

air and stone landscape
air layer in gaps between crushed stones

summer: open + mesh
When the wooden doors and windows are opened, wind travels through the upper and lower floors. Furthermore, the house copes with high temperature and humidity because the gaps in the wooden roof structure and the crushed stones are ventilated.

upper floor of guest house

lower floor of main house

section

winter: closed
When the wooden doors and windows are closed, the upper floor becomes an insulating air space above the lower floor. When the snow is piled up on the crushed stones, it acts like a snow cave. Thus, the main space of the lower floor is protected by many insulating layers of air.

upper floor of guest house

lower floor of main house

Above The roof is a single plane that combines a top layer of glazing over wood and air spaces to insulate certain areas and admit daylight and heat to others. The glazing permits snow to adhere to the roof for increased insulation in winter. The crushed stone, in conjunction with the sectional organization of spaces, accounts for seasonal differences. In winter, the stone protects against cold air currents through the "snow cave" phenomenon, and in summer, it cools incoming air for ventilation.

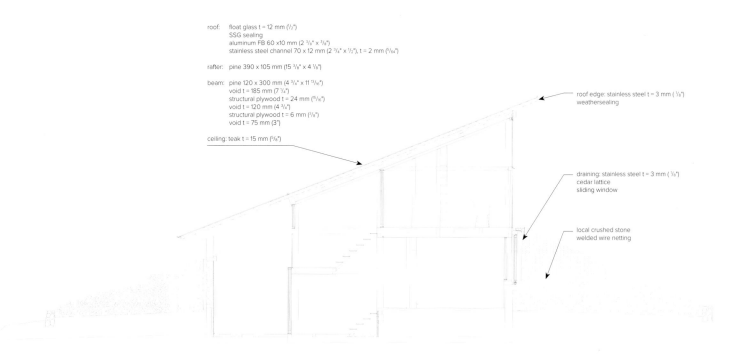

roof: float glass t = 12 mm (1/2")
SSG sealing
aluminum FB 60 x10 mm (2 3/8" x 3/8")
stainless steel channel 70 x 12 mm (2 3/4" x 1/2"), t = 2 mm (5/64")

rafter: pine 390 x 105 mm (15 3/8" x 4 1/8")

beam: pine 120 x 300 mm (4 3/4" x 11 13/16")
void t = 185 mm (7 1/4")
structural plywood t = 24 mm (15/16")
void t = 120 mm (4 3/4")
structural plywood t = 6 mm (3/8")
void t = 75 mm (3")

ceiling: teak t = 15 mm (5/8")

roof edge: stainless steel t = 3 mm (1/8")
weathersealing

draining: stainless steel t = 3 mm (1/8")
cedar lattice
sliding window

local crushed stone
welded wire netting

Opposite The terrace rests above the primary living quarters, which are lit by window wells in the rock. Welded wire provides a clear-cut form around the openings by holding the stones in place, much like gabions. Despite some additional reinforcement, most of the stone remains exposed on the incline.

Above The design involved methodical planning. Program was arranged horizontally and vertically according to hourly frequency of use, ventilation and natural light requirements, as well as thermal variation.

**Balmori Associates,
Green Roofs at the Solaire Building,
New York, New York, United States**

Landscape architects Balmori Associates collaborated with Pelli Clarke Pelli Architects to integrate vegetated roofs and a hydrological system into the Solaire Building, the first sustainable residential high-rise in the United States. Two green roofs—a 5,000-square-foot (464.5 square-meter) terrace on the nineteenth floor and a 4,800-square-foot (445.9 square-meter) roof on the twenty-eighth floor—absorb rainwater and filter pollutants from the excess runoff, which is collected in a basement cistern together with the building's gray water. This water is later reused to irrigate not only the Solaire roofs but local parks as well.

Above Right Typically, green roofs are not meant to function as rooftop gardens. The intensive vegetated surface of the large terrace, however, offers the building's residents desirable outdoor green space, with views of Battery Park City and the Hudson River.

Right Bamboo groves screen the views of and sounds from the mechanical equipment. Additionally, they create shade and reduce wind at the seating areas and along the walkways.

Opposite The vegetated surfaces of Solaire merge architecture, urban setting, and landscape: Here the gleaming sculptural forms of ventilation units that line a walkway of stone pavers are continued by the buildings in the distance. At the same time, in the dense urban fabric of lower Manhattan, greens roofs, especially when clustered, contribute to the environment by absorbing solar radiation and improving air quality.

Opposite Below Three types of planting beds form terraces rising from the paths and benches at the periphery of the roof. The two categories of vegetated roofs at the Solaire use different plants. The extensive green roof consists of grasses and sedums in 4 inches (102 millimeters) of planting soil. Nine floors below, the intensive green terrace displays a larger variety of flora, including bamboo and other perennials, in 4-, 12-, and 18-inch (102-, 305-, and 457-millimeter) planting beds.

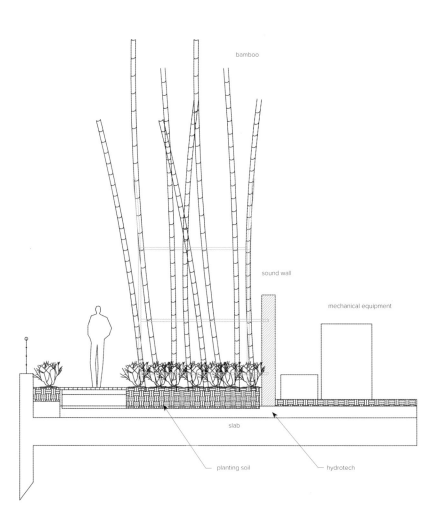

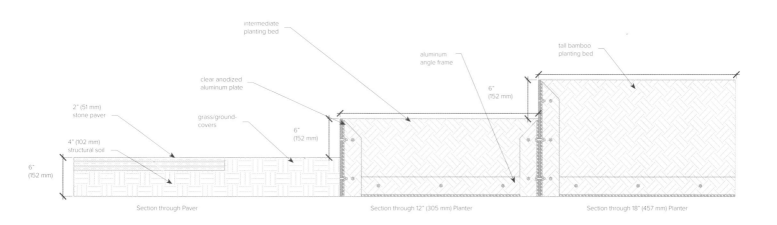

intermediate
planting bed

aluminum
angle frame

tall bamboo
planting bed

clear anodized
aluminum plate

2" (51 mm)
stone paver

grass/ground-
covers

6"
(152 mm)

6"
(152 mm)

4" (102 mm)
structural soil

6"
(152 mm)

Section through Paver

Section through 12" (305 mm) Planter

Section through 18" (457 mm) Planter

Conservation of Resources

"Conservation of Resources" examines dwellings whose architecture significantly reduces both the consumption of natural resources and the production of waste or pollutants. Two targets of conservation—energy and water—form logical divisions for this section. Energy use faces the dual threat that the planet will run out of fossil fuels before renewable sources completely replace them and that the greenhouse gases produced from their consumption will cause irreparable damage. An additional consideration is the destructive process of extracting fossil fuels. A similar problem confronts water usage: there is a need both to conserve this natural and cyclical resource and to prevent its contamination.

Nearly all the projects in "Alternative Energy Sources" rely on solar technologies to generate electricity and heat for hot water. For the high-density housing communities of BedZED and the Solarsiedlung, centralized plants devoted to energy and water storage or sewage treatment can sustain the entire development of housing, offices, and services. Housing at BedZED consists of zero-energy buildings, a term that refers to the zero net energy consumption in a single year. Energy produced onsite through BedZED's photovoltaic system and from tree-waste fuel yields a balanced equation with energy consumed. Housing at the Solarsiedlung consists of plus-energy buildings. That is, the system produces more energy than the complex can use and so is fed back to the local utility grid—exceeding the minimal impact of most sustainable homes. The overall consideration of this section is not active technologies themselves, but the ideal of a self-sustaining home. Thus, the Port Perry House appears here, even though it does not generate renewable energy. Unlike houses such as the Eastern Sierra Residence, which achieves self-sufficiency through a combination of active and passive methods, Port Perry is remarkable because its integration of multiple passive strategies results in near independence in a cold climate without recourse to fossil fuels.

In incorporating renewable energy into a home, designers face a challenge in the amount of equipment that they must add to the structure. The engineering technologies of most renewable systems tend to determine the architectural appearance, construction, and detailing of the building envelope. At the Solar Umbrella Residence, the photovoltaic panels are indeed an additional layer to the building envelope; however, the architects seamlessly worked the panels into the design as a roof canopy. Adhered to the standing seam metal roof of the Eastern Sierra Residence, photovoltaic laminates—strips of polymer containing thin-film amorphous silicon solar cells—eliminate brackets and panels and require simpler electrical connections. The solar cells laminated between glazing panels at BedZED are especially building-integrated: the solar panels form part of the wall and roof fenestration and appear from the interior as a light-filtering screen. To counter the perception of sustainable systems as an optional and costly add-on, designers are focusing on ways to integrate technologies into the building material. Some products, like solar shingles, are currently available and some, like solar cell sprays or infrared-sensitive films, are in development. The idea is that, rather than a separate category, sustainability must fully become a part of the design language.

The water conservation methods featured in "Hydrological Systems" transcend the customary low-flow shower heads and water-saving appliances standard in most homes today. Overall, aside from black water sewage processing, water conservation measures may be integrated into residential architecture with little added cost. Rainwater collection is the simplest way to conserve resources; indeed, the harvesting of rainwater has long been practiced in the arid regions of the world. Typically, the roof of a home functions as a collector, funneling the water into a storage tank. In A House for the Future, an unusually large gutter fabricated as part of the green roof and eaves serves as the storage container. Green roofs or water collection systems, the latter cleverly informing the design of the Residence on Beverly Skyline, help to reduce storm water runoff in areas with few porous surfaces or a danger of soil erosion. The soil and vegetation on a green roof also filter the rainwater, which may contain chemical and organic contaminants, diverting it from the groundwater. Furthermore, using the filtered water for irrigation or utility needs within the home diminishes dependence on the municipal water supply or groundwater wells.

At the opposite end of the use cycle, the C2C Home exemplifies the conservation of wastewater from the kitchen, shower, and laundry, as well as effluence from the toilets. Treated to eradicate microorganisms, gray water can be reused within the home for flushing toilets; untreated, gray water contains nutrients beneficial to plants and is used for irrigation. Black water recycling requires a more involved system of filters and biological treatment to render the water free of contaminants before discharging it into the environment. The C2C Home puts black water to ideal reuse as fertilizer and irrigation on site. (A similar system is installed at the Port Perry House.) Biofiltering of waste will also free the house from connecting to the overburdened local sewage system. Designed for A House for the Future, but never built—as it requires constant use to operate effectively and the house is not continually occupied— a constructed wetlands system employing a reed bed would have allowed for the natural filtering of wastewater.

Energy efficient and nonpolluting, water applied to heating and cooling provides another way to reduce dependency on nonrenewable energy sources. Like other homes in this volume, the McKinley Residence takes advantage of solar energy to heat water for the radiant floor system. The Water Villa demonstrates how water serves for cooling. The hydrological system is particularly convenient for the floating villa given its water environment; but a similar method, a geothermal heat pump for heating or cooling water that has been extracted from an underground aquifer, forms the basis of the building systems of many land-based homes, such as the Great Bay and Oxford Gardens Residences seen earlier.

Of course, other renewable sources are available to architects, including power harnessed from the wind. At BedZED, for instance, wind drives the passive ventilation stack system, which recovers heat from outgoing stale air. Whatever the source, many governments, beginning at the municipal level, have begun to legislate energy efficiency. For homeowners, tax credits, rebates, and exemptions may be another benefit of efficient building systems and renewable energy use. The projects throughout this section, even if ideal examples of self-sufficiency, provide tangible and architecturally complementary methods of conservation.

Alternative Energy Sources

**Arkin-Tilt Architects,
Eastern Sierra Residence, Gardnerville,
Nevada, United States**

Passive and active technologies come
together to create an energy-efficient and
environmentally responsive home in a hot,
arid climate with cold winter winds, east of
the Sierra Nevada Mountain range. In this
region of the United States, which on average
sees over three hundred sunny days a year,
solar energy is ideal. On the south side of
the house, an angled row of seven collector
panels carry a heat-absorbing fluid to a heat
exchanger. The tubes then form loops in sand
beds under the floor plate of the home to
warm the interior space through radiation.
No fossil fuels are required.

Above Integrated photovoltaic laminates are installed on the sloped standing seam metal roof to provide electricity for the house. Additionally, rows of photovoltaic cells form a shaded pergola for the terrace. The support brackets are adjustable, so the panels may be rotated to catch seasonal sun angles and help shed the build-up of snow. The photovoltaic system is linked to a grid intertie inverter, which connects the system to the utility grid and returns power it to when the house generates a surplus.

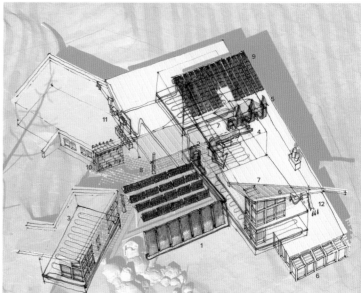

1 solar hot water collectors	7 glass floor tiles for daylight
2 heat exchange for domestic hot water	8 PV array shades trellis
3 thermal storage sand bed	9 roof-integrated PV laminates
4 night flush cooling	10 trombe wall warms batteries
5 high clerestory ventilation	11 inverters connect to grid
6 passive solar heat gain	12 greenhouse adds humidity

Left The center of the complex—comprising the house, attached guestroom, garage, and storage area—shelters a terrace whose small pond provides some relief from the dry environment. A trombe wall, backdrop for the pond, heats the storage area and prevents the batteries for the backup power system from freezing during the winter. The panels of the trombe wall are made of salvaged glass, overlapped in rows like shingles.

Pugh + Scarpa Architecture, Solar Umbrella Residence, Venice, California

In the spirit of Paul Rudolph's Umbrella House of 1953, Solar Umbrella elegantly reinterprets the strategy of a solar canopy for thermal protection in a hot, sunny climate. The canopy combines function, form, and spatial experience. The solar panels, an active technology typically applied to buildings in a strictly utilitarian approach, become an essential component in the composition of interlocking solids and voids, transparency and layering.

Above The master bedroom on the second floor opens onto a generous outdoor terrace overlooking the garden. This space is sheltered by the solar canopy and a screen on the front elevation, defining an outdoor room that is integrated with the volume of the house, much in the tradition of California modernist architecture.

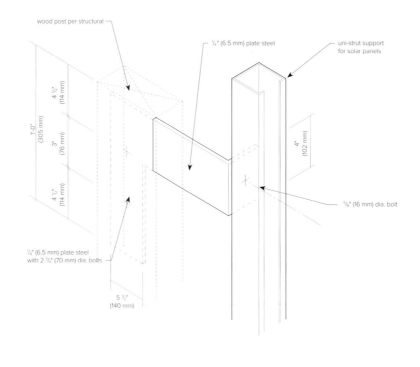

wood post per structural

¼" (6.5 mm) plate steel

uni-strut support
for solar panels

4 ½"
(114 mm)

1'-0"
(305 mm)

3"
(76 mm)

4 ½"
(114 mm)

4"
(102 mm)

⅝" (16 mm) dia. bolt

¼" (6.5 mm) plate steel
with 2 ¾" (70 mm) dia. bolts

5 ½"
(140 mm)

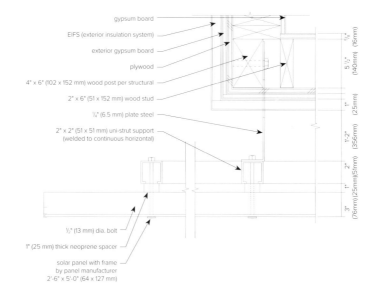

gypsum board

EIFS (exterior insulation system)

exterior gypsum board

plywood

4" x 6" (102 x 152 mm) wood post per structural

2" x 6" (51 x 152 mm) wood stud

¼" (6.5 mm) plate steel

2" x 2" (51 x 51 mm) uni-strut support
(welded to continuous horizontal)

½" (13 mm) dia. bolt

1" (25 mm) thick neoprene spacer

solar panel with frame
by panel manufacturer
2'-6" x 5'-0" (64 x 127 mm)

⅝" (16mm)

5 ½" (140mm)

1" (25mm)

1'-2" (356mm)

2" (51mm)

1" (25mm)

3" (76mm)

Above An axonometric detail reveals the straightforward connection between solar panel and wall structure. A plan detail shows the assembly by which the eighty-nine solar panels (manufactured by BP Solar) are mounted to the vertical structure. The design takes advantage of the compressed profile of amorphous thin film silicon. Theoretically, this type of cost-effective solar cell could be integrated directly into the building envelope, which would improve conversion efficiencies.

Opposite Wrapping the south elevation and roof of the house, the canopy of photovoltaic panels not only screens the building from direct solar radiation, thus preventing excessive thermal heat gain, but also absorbs the intense sunlight and converts it into electricity. In fact, the house derives all of its electrical requirements from solar energy.

**Breathe Architects,
Port Perry House,
Port Perry, Ontario, Canada**

The architect likens the house to an efficient machine that conserves resources. Although this residence relies primarily on passive technologies, its efficiency is such that it requires no furnace and thus avoids burning fossil fuels. Instead, the building envelope and structure provide interior conditioning suited to both winter and summer temperatures. Two levels of green roofs (the upper is hidden by the angle of view) absorb solar radiation so that the interior remains cool in summer. Rainwater is also absorbed to prevent excess runoff into Chalk Lake below. In addition, a biofilter system on site treats waste water.

Above The large south-facing curtain wall forms the main aperture for admitting solar radiation. Compact and cubic in form, the 28 × 28-foot (8.5 × 8.5-meter) house is simple to heat and ventilate. Vines will be grown up the walls to shade the house in summer and deflect wind in winter.

Left The stairwell serves as a solar chimney, which ventilates the house as the updraft of warm air draws cool air in at the bottom. R40 insulation is maintained on the roofs. The open plan and section promote air circulation—in fact, the only separate room is a toilet enclosure. Solar hot water panels were installed on the upper roof instead of the window wall as originally planned due to partial shading from tall trees.

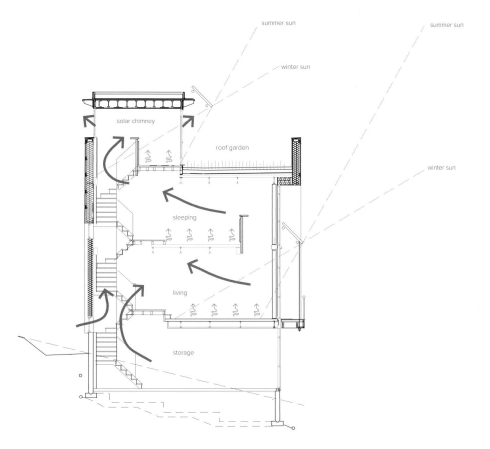

Above Windows on the north, east, and west sides are modestly sized to provide sufficient light and views but prevent heat loss. The wall construction consists of plywood floor joists run vertically to a height of 25 feet (7.6 meters) to form a hybrid balloon-framed curtain wall; it maintains an insulation value of R40 throughout because the floors do not penetrate the walls but are supported by a post-and-beam structure within. The thick walls, filled with cellulose insulation, are clad with a prefinished birch plywood rainscreen.

Above Left Windows are triple glazed with a low-e coating and gas fill to admit daylight and reflect solar radiation as part of the house's "mass under glass" system. The parallam post-and-beam frame rests on metal columns just inside the building envelope.

Above The concrete floors store heat from sunlight coming through the large south window and release it at night. On colder and overcast days, the radiant in-floor heating system warms the house. During the winter, the utility service (from which the owners have elected to buy renewable power only) supplies just 8 percent of the house's energy needs; the rest is generated by the house itself.

**Bill Dunster Architects,
Beddington Zero Energy Development
(BedZED), Hackbridge, Sutton,
United Kingdom**

BedZED launches sustainable lifestyles and
building systems at the scale of the housing
estate. The architect's mandate is to reduce
the average household's yearly carbon emissions output (typically occurring through
energy use, vehicular use, and food sourcing)
and thus its ecological footprint. The design
retains the qualities of a garden village, while
establishing sufficient density for a thriving
sustainable community—a model that could
greatly reduce urban sprawl and increase the
quality of life. This development in a south
London borough, which includes a mix of
eighty-two housing units, workspaces, an office park, and shared leisure and sports facili-
ties, introduces the idea of "solar urbanism"
to the design of the terraced row house.

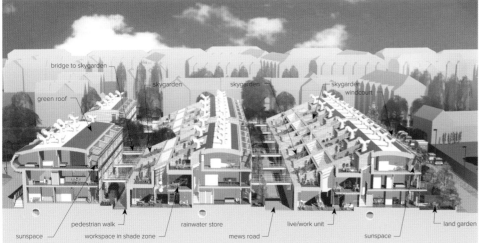

bridge to skygarden

skygarden

skygarden

skygarden

green roof

windcourt

pedestrian walk

sunspace

workspace in shade zone

rainwater store

mews road

live/work unit

sunspace

land garden

Above Wind scoops with colorful vanes capture the breeze for the wind-driven ventilation stacks. The heat recovery system preheats incoming fresh air throughout the buildings using heat from outgoing stale air. The system omits a fan-assisted mechanical system, which would increase efficiency but carbon emissions as well. The passive ventilation system is one of the features of the ZED in a Box standard housing type (based on the BedZED model) that the firm is selling as a carbon-neutral housing kit to introduce sustainability to the construction and development industry.

Left A section through the three rows of terraced houses reveals dwellings of different sizes, ranging from a studio flat to a three-bedroom maisonette, as well as live/work units to discourage vehicular use. All of the residences have access to either sunspaces or an outdoor garden. Circulation through the complex includes both a narrow mews road and a pedestrian walk.

Right The development makes the most of passive design strategies that greatly decrease the overall demand for heat, enabling the entire community to meet its energy needs through renewable sources alone. A large glazed façade runs along the south side of the three rows of homes, warming the sunspaces within, which have floors and walls of high thermal mass. The superinsulated triple-glazed windows provide abundant natural light, and in the evening, the interiors are illuminated with energy-efficient artificial lighting. Other passive measures, such as natural stack ventilation and energy-efficient appliances, contribute as well.

Opposite All photovoltaic panels are integrated into the glazing system on the south façades and terrace roofs. Laminated between glass, they appear as a seamless part of the design. Sufficient solar energy is generated throughout the development to run forty small electric vehicles intended for carpooling. A power plant on the site provides other heating and power needs and is fueled by 850 metric tons (937 tons) of woodchip per year. The woodchip is sourced from a regional urban tree station, which collects tree waste from two south metropolitan boroughs, converting to fuel a valuable resource that would otherwise be sent to landfills.

**Architekturbüro Rolf Disch,
Solarsiedlung at Schlierberg,
Freiburg, Germany**

The fundamental concept driving the design
of this sustainable community is to use
natural resources for all energy, construction, building, and transportation systems.
Rows of fifty-eight "plus-energy" houses and
a mixed-use block are closely grouped to create sheltered outdoor spaces and to encourage social interaction. The terraced rows are
oriented along the east-west axis so that the
inclined roofs, consisting of photovoltaic
panels, capture the southern sun throughout
the seasons.

Above and Left The long form of the Sonnenschiff (literally, "Sun Ship"), with its mix of commercial and office spaces below and penthouses above, shields the row houses from the main road and creates an entrance front for the Solarsiedlung. Thermal vacuum tube collectors on the building provide hot water for the entire community, and a centralized woodchip station generates power for electricity and heat. To further reduce the reliance on fossil fuels, residents are encouraged to share cars, ride bicycles, and take public transportation. Conservation extends to water consumption as well: Rainwater is collected and reused to irrigate gardens and to flush toilets, while runoff is discharged above ground in swales incorporated into the landscaping.

Opposite The sheltering photovoltaic roof panels supply additional electricity to the community. All of the passive technologies contribute to energy savings; however, the homes actually generate more energy than they consume—hence the term "plus-energy." Excess energy is returned to the utility grid, providing a profit to the residents. The two- to three-story units are fairly standard as they are based on a modular system; finish colors and external features such as the spiral stair add diversity.

Above In each of the row houses, the living spaces are located on the south, while service rooms like the kitchen and baths are on the north. All mechanical services are concentrated in a central machinery canal serving the row. Using prefabricated wood components allowed a measure of precision in construction while keeping the on-site work efficient and costs lower. The exterior wall has a thick, 400-millimeter (16-inch) profile with an interior timber frame that minimizes thermal bridges. In addition, rather than interrupt the continuous insulation within the wall, utilities such as water pipes are housed in heavy timber baseboard circuits.

biofiltration, gray and black water treatment, cooling loop, rainwater collection, hydronic radiant floor heating

Hydrological Systems

Coates Design with Tim Meldrum, C2C Home, Roanoke, Virginia, United States

The winning entry for the Cradle to Cradle Home Design and Construction Competition will be built on an infill lot, to join a series of other entries that began construction in 2005. The design evolved from a new consideration of the idea of the hearth and is centered on a core that serves all the essential systems of the house, including rainwater collection, black and gray water treatment, ventilation, thermal storage, and daylighting. The core will be clad in a superconductive, photosynthetic plasma cell material based on spinach protein, but until this experimental technology is available, the core remains a solar chimney and heat sink.

Above The structure is set into the low incline of the land, which slopes to the street. A play area with groundcovers among a grid of pavers leads to the house. On one side, a landscape of native plants replaces the usual front lawn; on the other, a row of planters is irrigated by treated wastewater from the house. The vegetables cultivated in these beds complete the cycle of use and production.

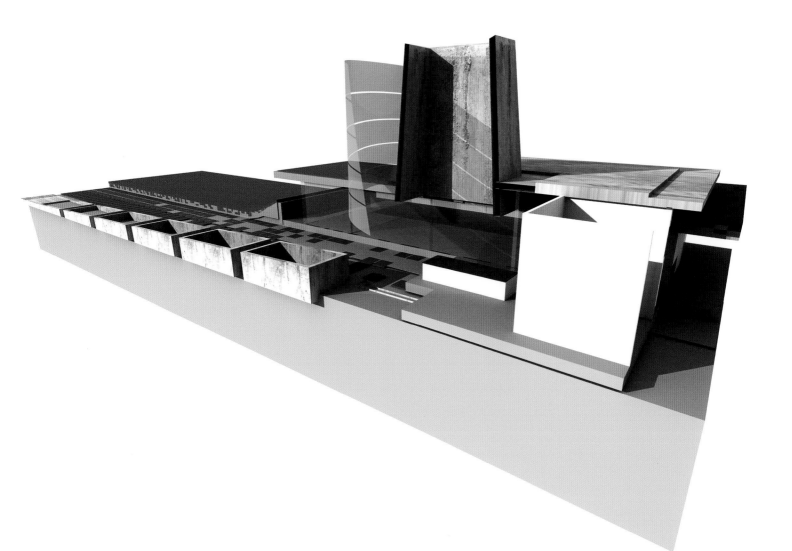

Above One wall of the main core is the house's wet stack (the blue block in the rendering). All household plumbing fixtures are located on either side of the wall, which also holds the rainwater collected and filtered by the green roof system. Stored in a tank, the harvested water is used for flushing toilets and other nonpotable functions as well as subsurface irrigation for the plantings. Thus, the house relies on municipal water only for consumption and bathing and requires no connection to the public sewer.

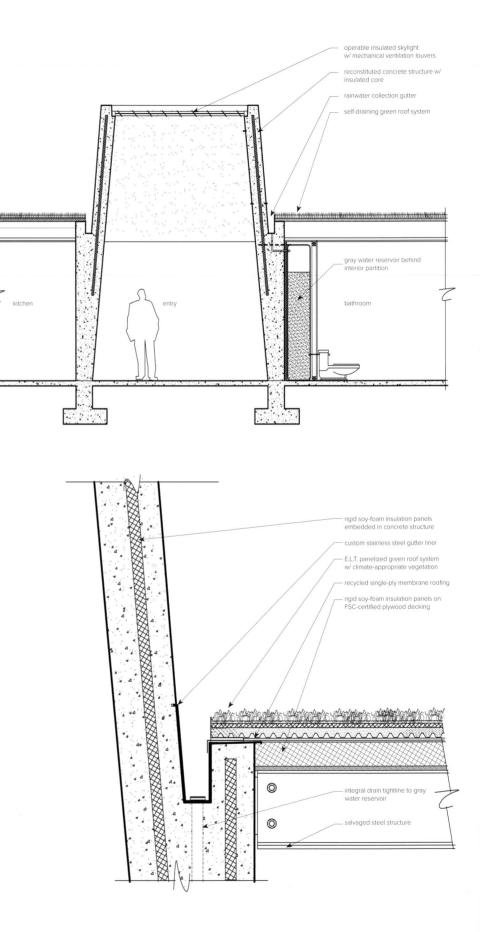

operable insulated skylight
w/ mechanical ventilation louvers

reconstituted concrete structure w/
insulated core

rainwater collection gutter

self-draining green roof system

gray water reservoir behind
interior partition

kitchen

entry

bathroom

rigid soy-foam insulation panels
embedded in concrete structure

custom stainless steel gutter liner

E.L.T. panelized green roof system
w/ climate-appropriate vegetation

recycled single-ply membrane roofing

rigid soy-foam insulation panels on
FSC-certified plywood decking

integral drain tightline to gray
water reservoir

salvaged steel structure

Above and Right Environmental materials are incorporated into the house wherever possible, such as soy-foam insulation, salvaged steel for the structure, and recycled membrane roofing. The skylight at the top of the core has photovoltaic, servo-actuated ventilation louvers.

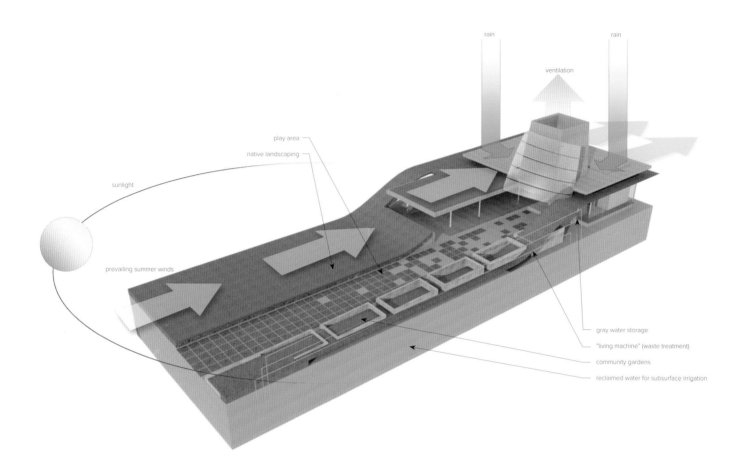

rain

rain

ventilation

play area

native landscaping

sunlight

prevailing summer winds

gray water storage

"living machine" (waste treatment)

community gardens

reclaimed water for subsurface irrigation

Above Underground, a filtration system treats household effluence biologically and percolates the black water through graduated layers of gravel and soil under the planters to nourish the gardens. The system accommodates wastewater from adjacent houses as well. Just as communal waste is treated, excess energy generated by the photosynthetic skin in the future will be shared.

**Jestico + Whiles,
A House for the Future, St. Fagans,
Cardiff, Wales, United Kingdom**

The vegetated roof curves down on the
north side of the house to a large and deep
metal gutter used for collecting and storing
rainwater. In fact, this outsized container is
capable of holding more than 3 cubic meters
(105.9 cubic feet) of water. Based on the average rainfall in the region and the roof surface
area, the architects have calculated that the
house collects approximately 56 cubic meters
(1,977.6 cubic feet) of rain each year. This
quantity represents the conservation of about
a quarter of the water used by an average
four-person household in Wales.

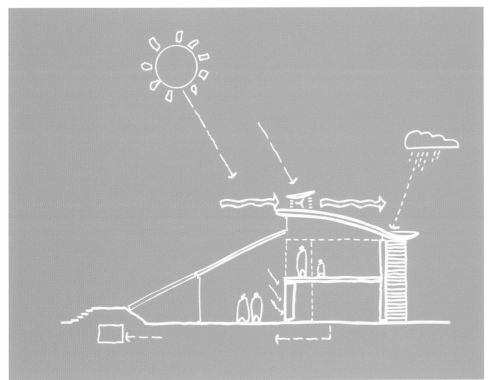

Above and Left Planted with sedum, the green roof helps filter some of the rainwater but also absorbs solar radiation and carbon dioxide in the air. Sedum is often employed on these extensive green roofs for its shallow root system. The stored water passes through a filter for nonpotable uses within the house, such as flushing toilets and doing laundry. Appliances such as the washing machine or dishwasher accordingly meet low energy and water consumption requirements. On the opposite side of the house, the rainwater flows down the slope to a gutter, where it is channeled to the garden in front.

Bercy Chen Studio, Residence on Beverly Skyline, Austin, Texas, United States

The focus of the design was to connect the house with the site, a garden of indigenous plants located on a steep gradient with a creek at the foot of the slope. The result is an architectural intervention that addresses conditions in the humid subtropical climate by collecting rainwater in pools at the ground floor of the house and channeling it down the slope to a storage tank near the creek. The system alleviates runoff from thunderstorms that can cause flash flooding in lower parts of the city. The harvested rainwater is then used to irrigate the garden and will provide water for an intended outdoor shower.

Above In the evening, as the garden below disappears in the darkness, the illuminated pools form a dramatic foreground to distant panoramic views. The glazed walls fold open and stack to the side so that the pools become part of the living space. With the built-in seating, nothing mediates between the inhabitants and the calming presence of the flowing water.

Left Water rushes through a tube from the upper level to one of the cascading pools that wrap around the sides of the house. The pools are constructed with poured-in-place concrete and salvaged steel sheets.

garage

rainwater cistern

creek

Above and Opposite The harvested rainwater is pumped back uphill to recirculate through the pools and the Xeriscape, or water-conserving, garden, which is planted with Carolina wolfberry, red yucca, and Mexican buckeye—species native to the region. The design of the garden reflects the local landscape and preserves the natural qualities of the site.

**David Hertz Architects,
McKinley Residence Addition,
Venice, California, United States**

Photovoltaic panels and flat-plate collectors form a low profile on the flat roofs of the house; in particular, the pool house where the roof tapers to a thin knife edge at the eaves. The addition forms an L that wraps around an outdoor court with a lap pool. Designed to be energy efficient as well as responsive to environmental and health concerns, the pool uses a silver-based ionization system that greatly reduces chlorine levels.

Above Left Three different solar energy systems contribute to the home's utilities. While photovoltaic panels generate most of the house's electrical requirements and the flat-plate collectors supply water to the heating system, other hot water needs are met through evacuated tube collectors that concentrate solar energy with small parabolic troughs.

Above Right Flat-plate collectors on the roof generate hot water for the in-floor radiant heating system. Solar energy heats the water in the pipes of the collectors, which is then circulated through the hot water tank into the tubes of the radiant system in the concrete and Syndecrete floors.

**Architectuurstudio Herman Hertzberger,
Water Villa, Middelburg, Netherlands**

The Water Villa rests on a light hexagonal
flotation ring constructed of massive hollow
steel pipe at the waterfront of De Veersche
Poort. Specific factors determined the materials and construction of the flotation device:
the depth of the water; the possible draft, or
depth of the vessel's keel below the water's
surface when loaded; and tidal or other
changes in water levels. In this instance, the
steel flotation system is suited to the stable
water level and the need for a shallow draft,
but other technologies could be applied in
different water environments.

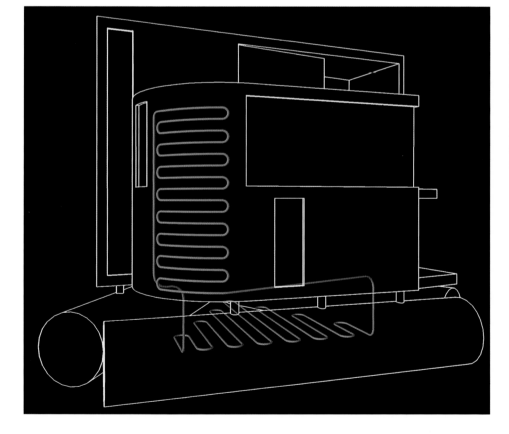

Left As an added convenience, water from the site can be used in the villa's cooling system. An environmental closed-circuit system, however, will be available for future villas. To counteract heat gain, a loop runs from the underside of the house, where the water temperature remains cooler than air and surface temperatures, to the walls and roof. The location of the cooling system corresponds approximately to the diagram, although the flotation base has developed into a ring.

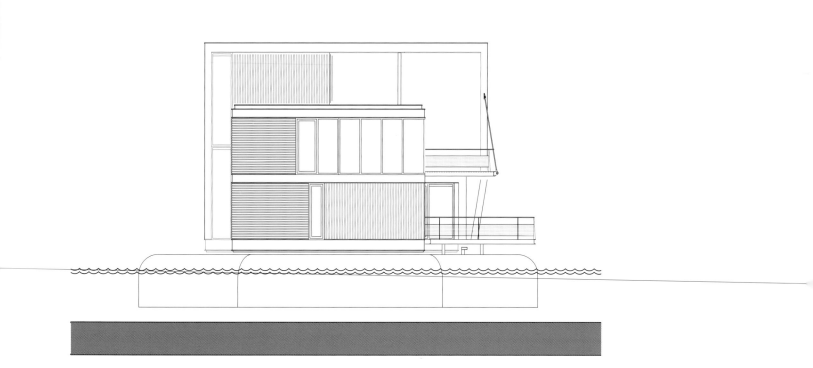

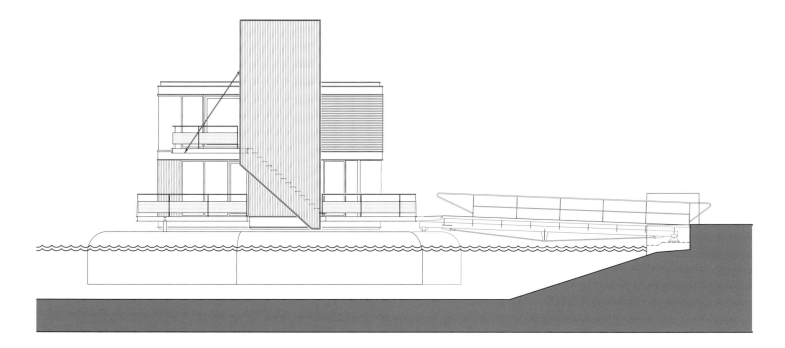

Opposite The steel offshore pipes have an upturned D-shaped profile over 2 meters (6.6 feet) in width and height, with a protective exterior finish that requires minimal maintenance. The ring is capable of supporting a total weight of 135 tons (148.8 metric tons) in water.

Above Left The hollow interior of the floating base facilitates the addition of ballast to attain the required depth in the water and to adjust the building's balance. As well, it provides an immense amount of space for storage.

Use of Building Materials

No study of sustainable residential space can exclude environmentally responsible materials. The projects in "Use of Building Materials" are significant not because they incorporate as many sustainable materials as possible, but for how they experiment with new composites or introduce ingenious applications for more common materials. Many of the recycled elements are not even specifiable manufactured products. All these works are attentive to the sourcing of construction materials, similar in intent to the locally sourced products of the "Bioregionalism" projects, but emphasizing the issues of embodied energy and cost. Also, all the architects chose materials with low VOC levels and minimal or no off-gassing to provide a cleaner, nontoxic living space inside and to prevent contamination of the soil and water outside. New and used form the two basic divisions here: "Elemental and Experimental Materials" presents recently developed materials as well as reinterpretations of more traditional or rudimentary ones, while "Salvaged and Recycled Materials" examines how architects integrate used materials and entire post-consumer objects into a living environment, creating a sort of architectural bricolage.

A staple of vernacular construction, elemental materials like straw and bamboo are making a reappearance in architect-designed sustainable homes, often in a whole, minimally processed form, as demonstrated in the Great (Bamboo) Wall and the Straw House. Applicable wherever the plant may be cultivated, they are not limited to traditional methods of construction. Renewable materials like these are popular since they may be easily regrown and are consequently not endangered as a resource. The use of wood, however, brings with it a necessary caution: the awareness of its production source. Standards for the responsible sourcing of wood products, such as that set by the Forest Stewardship Council in the United States, assure that certified wood excludes endangered or genetically modified species and wood originating from tree farms or plantations that have replaced natural forests—a process that destroys the natural ecosystems within.

Just as renewability has become a prerequisite for many architects in specifying construction materials, the embodied energy of materials has emerged as another factor intrinsic to sustainability. Embodied energy is the total sum of energy associated with the life cycle of a material, from the extraction of raw material, through the processing, manufacturing, transport, use, and disposal of the finished product. Although metal has a higher embodied energy due to its extensive manufacturing procedures, steel's structural strength, durability, and reusability make it a natural choice for many projects. In the homes here that employ metal as a primary material—the Turbulence House and the Annie Street and Slavin-Arnholz Residences—these factors plus its low maintenance counterbalance the greater embodied energy. For the first two projects, the steel structure is also a precision material that can be assembled from a kit of parts with specific quantities and dimensions, allowing for greater efficiency and substantially reducing waste.

Newer innovations, such as the laminated bamboo lumber of the Bamboo Furniture House and the Syndecrete of the McKinley Residence, were developed—through the initiative of the architects—to fill a need for practical structural and surfacing elements made from widely available raw materials: in the first case, renewable and native, and in the second, part postconsumer waste. These new products offer a potentially wider range of applications and greater utility than the less environmental products that they replace. Experimental materials are not without their trials, however. Working with local labor and suppliers proved more challenging than expected in building the Bamboo Furniture House, but the architect remains optimistic that the experiment will facilitate the adoption of this inexpensive renewable resource in modern construction, both in China, with its preponderance of heavy construction, and beyond.

"Salvaged and Recycled Materials" explores unique ways of reusing nonarchitectural elements or construction materials, diverted from the scrap heap or landfill. The two terms "salvaged" and "recycled" have, in fact, slightly different shades of meaning. Salvaging implies the reuse of whole elements that would otherwise be disposed of, while recycling implies newness, as a result of processing or extracting a material and reconfiguring it in another form. The projects in this last division take the idea of recycling to be a process by which the house itself becomes the new end-product, with salvaged materials as ingredients.

The Future Shack demonstrates the most literal reuse of an object without reprocessing. In general, a house is expected to last and to see many lives. The Future Shack represents a number of current developments in temporary housing that carries the assumed recyclability of a building a step further by transforming shipping containers into modular, transportable objects, capable of repeated use in locations across the globe. In three projects—the Residence on Beverly Skyline, Lucy's House, and the Big Dig House—salvaged materials form permanent and fundamental components for the building envelope or structure of the house. All the materials shown here fill both environmental and functional objectives. Even the whimsical details of airplane fins and ore-cart wheels at the Eastern Sierra Residence serve as shading and structural brackets. Both the Driggs Avenue Loft Renovation and the Big Dig House illustrate that adopting sustainable materials is not always a case of substituting renewable or reclaimed materials for unecological ones. Instead, these projects set up entirely new parameters in the design process, redefining expectations of structure or finishes in residential spaces. The Big Dig House is indeed an exploratory foray. Designed here as a single-family home, it is also a prototype for future buildings, including a multifamily housing block to be constructed from the same salvaged roadway materials. Applying atypical materials to the domestic context has many implications for housing, and the question arises of how these materials with unexpected properties might transform the way we dwell.

renewable, straw
bale, environmentally
sourced, low-VOC,
off-the-shelf,
postconsumer

Elemental and Experimental Materials

**Shigeru Ban Architects,
Bamboo Furniture House, Beijing, China**

For this house in a development outside
of Beijing, the architect chose bamboo, an
easily grown indigenous plant, to develop
new types of structural laminated lumber.
Inspired by the laminated bamboo plywood
commonly used for concrete framework, the
firm produced a prototype lumber, working
with a local factory that laminated bamboo
strips with glue. Laminated bamboo lumber
and plywood appear throughout the house:
as a modular framing system, as beams, and
as finishes on interior and exterior walls. The
woven assembly of the plywood imbues the
material with a deeply tactile quality.

Above The house employs a prefabricated, modularized partition system, made with laminated bamboo studs and laminated bamboo plywood surfaces. Most of the modules along the hall facing the courtyard double as the doors or backs of modular storage units. The result is a deep functional wall on either side of the court. In a few locations, the backs of these cabinets form the outside wall of the house, with exterior finish applied over waterproofing. The bamboo reads primarily as a horizontal zone between the lighter expanses of floor, ceiling, and sky beyond.

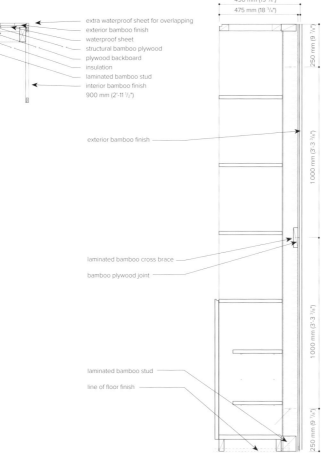

extra waterproof sheet for overlapping
exterior bamboo finish
waterproof sheet
structural bamboo plywood
plywood backboard
insulation
laminated bamboo stud
interior bamboo finish
900 mm (2'-11 ¹/₂")

490 mm (19 ¹/₄")
475 mm (18 ³/₄")

250 mm (9 ⁷/₈")

1,000 mm (3'-3 ³/₈")

exterior bamboo finish

laminated bamboo cross brace

bamboo plywood joint

1,000 mm (3'-3 ³/₈")

laminated bamboo stud

line of floor finish

250 mm (9 ⁷/₈")

Above and Left Modular panels line the outer walls of the house, where the texture more closely resembles that of vertical siding. The bamboo lumber prototype was tested to meet Japanese government standards, and its strength lies between that of timber and steel. In a part of the world where conventional lumber products are not readily available, the laminated bamboo lumber, once developed as an industry, would be inexpensive and make light construction a viable option for small structures.

Kengo Kuma Architects,
Great (Bamboo) Wall, Beijing, China

The design of the house investigates the material properties of the bamboo cane and its architectural use on a number of levels, the metaphoric included. Its lightness and its smooth, subtly varied surface makes the cane ideal as a screen and a filter between the natural and built realms. Reinforced-concrete cores fill the hollow interiors of larger canes for the house's structural columns, maintaining a consistency of material.

Above An ecological imperative for this new Beijing neighborhood was to incorporate natural and locally sourced materials. Honoring the long tradition of bamboo elements in Asian homes, canes serve as a wall and ceiling finish throughout, as flooring in the bedrooms and lounge, and even as a washbasin in the guest bath. Locally quarried dark slate adds a sense of depth and solidity.

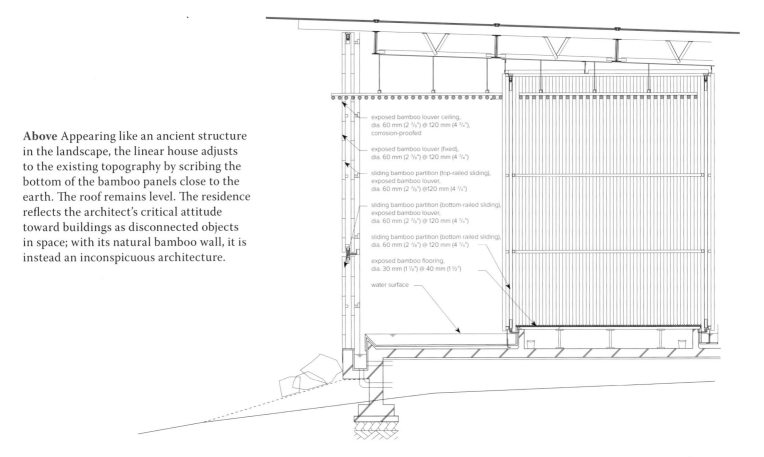

Above Appearing like an ancient structure in the landscape, the linear house adjusts to the existing topography by scribing the bottom of the bamboo panels close to the earth. The roof remains level. The residence reflects the architect's critical attitude toward buildings as disconnected objects in space; with its natural bamboo wall, it is instead an inconspicuous architecture.

exposed bamboo louver ceiling, dia. 60 mm (2 ³/₈") @ 120 mm (4 ³/₄"), corrosion-proofed

exposed bamboo louver (fixed), dia. 60 mm (2 ³/₈") @ 120 mm (4 ³/₄")

sliding bamboo partition (top-railed sliding), exposed bamboo louver, dia. 60 mm (2 ³/₈") @120 mm (4 ³/₄")

sliding bamboo partition (bottom-railed sliding), exposed bamboo louver, dia. 60 mm (2 ³/₈") @ 120 mm (4 ³/₄")

sliding bamboo partition (bottom railed sliding), dia. 60 mm (2 ³/₈") @ 120 mm (4 ³/₄")

exposed bamboo flooring, dia. 30 mm (1 ¹/₈") @ 40 mm (1 ½")

water surface

Above and Left Throughout the house, the bamboo partitions create varying degrees of screening: In reference to the Great Wall nearby, the bamboo walls connect rather than divide two sides. While most of the canes used in the partitions are 60 millimeters (2.36 inches) in diameter, the spacing of the canes changes the amount of light or separation from one room to another or from the exterior to the interior. Sliding screens overlap with fixed panels for a more solid, denser surface in the lounge and in other living spaces. The floor of the lounge consists of a smaller diameter whole cane.

Sarah Wigglesworth Architects, Straw House, North London, United Kingdom

A translucent rainscreen that ventilates the wall provides a window onto the straw bale infill that insulates half of the exterior walls of this home. Simple to handle and quickly installed, the bales are stacked between structural timber ladder frames. With their high insulative values, low embodied energy, recyclability, and low cost, straw bales represent a renewable material that holds great advantages over most present wall insulation and construction methods.

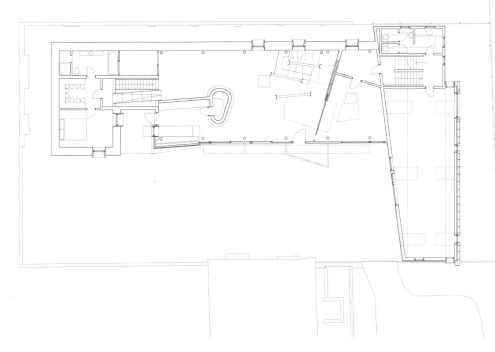

Above The house combines many passive environmental strategies that contribute to the unique composition of architectural elements and façades. Working in conjunction with the thermal mass provided by the straw bales, a large, glazed south wall admits sun to warm the living areas. The five-story library tower functions as a thermal chimney to ventilate the house. Another experimental cladding is being tested on the side façade of the office wing (visible on the right) in the form of a quilted fabric wall finish.

Left The straw bales, 465 millimeters (18.3 inches) deep line the north and west walls, wrapping around the bedrooms at the western end of the house. Each side of the linked home and office studio offers a material response to a specific site condition and orientation. The building combines agrarian and utilitarian materials, such as corrugated metal siding, that are unusual but highly applicable in an urban context.

Above The office façade forms a robust, industrial edge that contrasts with the lighter straw and rainscreen elevations. The east exterior wall is lined with sandbags for acoustic protection since it overlooks a railway line. The bags are filled with a hydraulic lime, cement, and sand mix. Gabion piers, containing recycled concrete from local demolition yards and enveloping structural concrete columns, support this wing—an engineering construction technique introduced to residential use. The design offers an investigation into low-tech and simply sourced construction materials, each of which the architects researched for potential life-cycle costs, toxicity, and embodied energy.

Above The interior walls of the house are finished with lime plaster, which adds fire protection on the straw bale sides. Other naturally finished materials include plywood doors. The bright, clean-edged interior belies the rusticity of the construction materials.

**Travis Price Architects,
Slavin-Arnholz Residence,
Washington D.C., United States**

Copper cladding, glass, and translucent fiberglass panels come together in the new addition. All materials incorporated into the home, especially on the exterior, are long-lasting and require little maintenance—a benefit in a four-story structure. The fiber-reinforced wall panels (Kalwall) may be well insulated without much loss of light and provide good thermal values. The translucent surface also helps in shading the interior.

Above Copper cladding on the addition adjoins the existing mottled brick walls of the house. Though dissimilar in scale and texture, the brick and copper share deep russet tones. The architect chose copper and steel for the exterior surfaces and structure because metals comprise embodied energy and are subject to minimal deterioration from the elements. Over time, the naturally weathering surface of the copper will impart an organic detail to the rectilinear forms of the house.

Above Right The top of the stair tower reaches a roof deck, where again a variety of materials are juxtaposed. Interior hardwoods are all sustainably sourced and only glass and natural stone tile are used.

Opposite The many decks facilitate natural ventilation throughout the house. Deck surfaces are a composite board, resistant to decay and requiring little upkeep. The wood and plastic compound is a mix of postconsumer recycled plastic and sawdust from waste wood. The copper cladding lends itself to many scales and treatments, including the ceilings of the porches.

**Bercy Chen Studio,
Residence on Annie Street,
Austin, Texas, United States**

The home incorporates a modular steel frame with an infill of thermally efficient, prefabricated and preinsulated steel panels, reducing construction site waste and making the tectonics of the building clear. Using an exposed structure with infill panels (faced with horizontal cumaru board) required fewer materials for the finishes inside and out. The steel is durable and both insect and decay resistant.

Above A number of factors contributed to the house's certification as a City of Austin Green Building project, including construction methods and materials. The home is a slab-on-grade building, with the sealed concrete slab serving as the finished floor. The concrete obviates additional layers of wood or nonrenewable materials, while eliminating dust and mold. Walls and ceilings are also efficiently constructed from clear stained seven-ply maple plywood. A flush glazed hallway pavilion between reflecting pools links the two halves of the house. Salvaged steel plates form the base of the pools, which are planted with native aquatics.

Steven Holl Architects,
Turbulence House,
Abiquiu, New Mexico, United States

Perched on a desert mesa, this artists' residence is constructed from intricately pieced together aluminum panels. The high reflectivity of the surface prevents the absorption of excess solar radiation and helps to cool the interior. To further reduce direct solar gain, the fenestration, which remains relatively small, is mostly located on the north or shaded sides of the house.

Opposite The house's aerodynamic form accommodates the desert wind through a central void on the ground level that gives the structure its two-legged appearance. (The smaller leg on the south side serves as a storage shed.) Natural finish, flat-lock seam aluminum panels form the shell of the house. The panels were designed using parametrics, then digitally fabricated by a sheet-metal company in Kansas City with extraordinary precision. The process minimizes waste material generated during production; excess aluminum can be recycled at the fabrication shop.

Above The prefabricated metal panels were bolted together on site, streamlining the construction process, further reducing waste materials, and leaving the land relatively undisturbed. The accuracy of the engineered assemblies kept construction time for the shell to two days.

Opposite The house consists of thirty-one metal panels with stressed skin and an aluminum rib structure. The largest panel is 8 × 22 feet (2.4 × 6.7 meters), a consequence of the 8-foot (2.4-meter) dimensional limitation of the standard 40-foot (12.2-meter) shipping container in which the material arrived at the site. Each panel, weighing an average of 7.5 pounds per square foot (36.6 kilograms per square meter), is uniquely shaped. All finishes are nontoxic and free of off-gassing from volatile organic compounds.

David Hertz Architects,
McKinley Residence Addition,
Venice, California, United States

The architect used the home as a laboratory for testing the application of many sustainable methods and materials, including the solid-surfacing material Syndecrete, which he developed. The cement-based compound incorporates up to 41 percent postindustrial and postconsumer recycled materials; including fly ash, carpet fiber, and ground or chipped metal, plastic, wood, and glass. Suitable for both exterior and interior applications, Syndecrete tiles form the pool decking in the courtyard and continue inside as the floor of the media room and pool house.

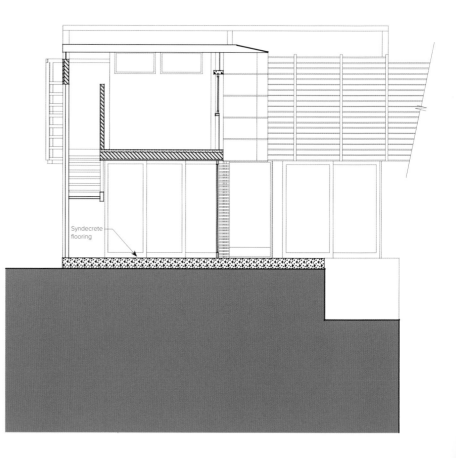

Syndecrete
flooring

Above Left This home showcases the natural appearance of Syndecrete, but it is available in other colors as well, ranging from nonpigmented (whitish) to pink to black. The surface is finished to reveal the aggregate, which varies according to the ingredients used. The designer intended the resultant terrazzolike appearance. The material is stable and, with no resins or polymers, does not release of chemicals into the air, or off-gas.

Above Right An outdoor solar shower features Syndecrete tile as an exterior wall cladding. Like other composite materials, it may also be precast into large forms. Developed for multiple uses, this reconstituted product can replace nonrenewable resources such as stone, and petroleum-based goods such as laminates and plastic composites. Other applications within the original and newer parts of the McKinley Residence include countertops, fireplaces, vanity basins, bathtubs, and showers.

reclamation, landfills, affordability, adaptive reuse, transformation, shipping containers, recyclable building

Salvaged and Recycled Materials

Matt Gagnon Studio,
Driggs Avenue Loft Renovation,
Brooklyn, New York, United States

The renovation of the loft space and redesign of the entrance as an anteroom to an informal gallery addresses sustainable design in a high-density urban context. The adaptive reuse of building space and construction materials represents environmentally focused choices rooted in the design process as opposed to the specifications. The project balances the partly cost-free materials with the additional labor required to assemble them, while greatly eliminating embodied energy from transport and waste. The eye-catching maple screen and coatrack are made of FSC-certified wood obtained from a local lumberyard.

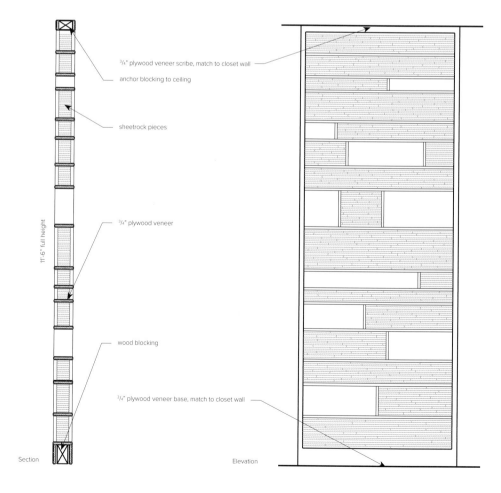

Above and Left Large amounts of gypsum wallboard left over from the removed partitions were cut down to pieces 6 inches (152 millimeters) deep and 24 or 36 inches (609 or 762 millimeters) long. These were stacked in a manner similar to stone wall construction, which relies on craft rather than a precise ordering. To minimize dust from the exposed gypsum, the finished wall is sealed with clear acrylic. Throughout the demolition and construction phases, no dumpster was needed: Excess materials like wall studs were advertised on Craig's List, and others were given away.

**Arkin-Tilt Architects,
Eastern Sierra Residence,
Gardnerville, Nevada, United States**

In addition to being energy efficient, this straw bale house incorporates many salvaged materials. Most striking are the ailerons—the hinged flaps on the wings of airplanes that control rolling movement—which have a second life as sun shades on the exterior of the greenhouse, a section of the home that is extensively glazed to receive solar radiation for thermal storage.

Above and Left Ore-cart wheels function as brackets to support trellis beams made from railroad track, in a reference to the region's long history of mining. Raised on both log timbers and slender metal posts, the trellis holds the canopy of adjustable photovoltaic cells that shades the terrace. Throughout, the house uses reclaimed wood for flooring, paneling, and decking, as well as recycled glass not only for the trombe wall but also for an aggregate countertop.

Bercy Chen Studio, Residence on Beverly Skyline, Austin, Texas, United States

The owner had obtained a large quantity of reclaimed glass block and wanted it incorporated into the renovation of the thirty-year-old house. Accordingly, the exterior was reclad with the glass block and wood rainscreen. As lighting conditions vary, even under overcast skies, the glass surface appears to be constantly shifting; at night, the façade glows as a block of white light.

Opposite The glass block creates a sense of light and openness that is reinforced by the many outdoor decks with transparent, frameless guardrails. The glass block is textured inside so that it transmits light but retains privacy for the interior, even where it faces the street. Large glazed openings throughout the house look out onto the garden and over the city.

**Rural Studio, Lucy's House,
Mason's Bend, Alabama, United States**

The building envelope of the main house
consists of stacked salvaged carpet tiles,
donated by Interface, a company that makes
widely distributed commercial carpeting.
Connected by the translucent entryway, the
folded metal structure adjacent contains the
parents' bedroom and sits above a tornado
shelter that also serves as a family room. The
transformation of this flooring product into
a construction material diverts the old carpet
from landfills; the energy that would have
gone into recycling it is turned to more productive effort, giving a nonrenewable material a second life. Subsequent to this project,
many flooring companies have introduced
reclaimed carpet products made into new or
reconditioned carpeting.

Above Using the carpet tiles for exterior walls required no additional finishes on either the interior or exterior, which amounts to a considerable savings in materials. The 72,000 pieces of carpet tile, stacked manually, are held in place by compression with a wood ring beam just below the eaves. Metal columns within the wall run from foundation to roof for structural support, since the stacked tiles do not have a load-bearing capacity. The broad eaves of the roof shelter the carpet walls from rain and sun.

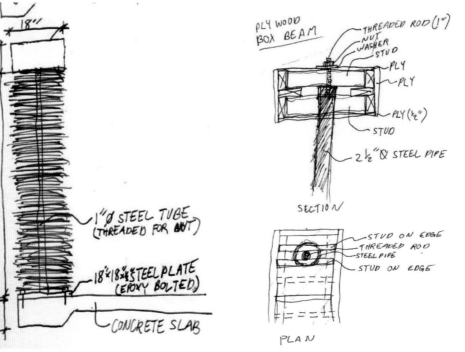

Above Right and Right Following a number of studies and mock-ups, the wall and its supporting structure were constructed in a total of three weeks time, with intermittent design and construction phases, somewhat akin to a fast-track project. The stacked carpet creates a subtly patterned and multicolored surface that has an welcoming tactility. The vermilion window sashes are set into thick, engineered wood frames, the laminations of which reflect the stacked pattern of the walls.

Above Synthetic carpeting has long been associated with indoor air-quality problems in working environments through off-gassing. Here, however, the salvaged tiles, reclaimed from office buildings throughout the United States, had all been manufactured over seven years ago. Thus the release of chemicals is negligible, and the family can enjoy a safe environment.

Sean Godsell Architects,
Future Shack, no fixed site

The Future Shack is a mass-produced dwelling that can be shipped throughout the world for many humanitarian applications, such as disaster relief, temporary shelter, and housing for developing nations. The design takes as its starting point recycled shipping containers. Their universality, durability, and low cost make them ideal for the structural shell of the house. Each unit includes a parasol roof that shades the top of the container from direct solar radiation and creates a protected outdoor space for the inhabitant.

Right The shelter is self-sufficient and may be assembled in twenty-four hours. In addition to the parasol, the module features water tanks, a solar power cell, a satellite receiver, a roof access ladder, and a container access ramp. Adjustable supports—a pair of brackets with telescoping legs that are attached to the exterior of the module—accommodate a variety of ground conditions, with little site preparation required.

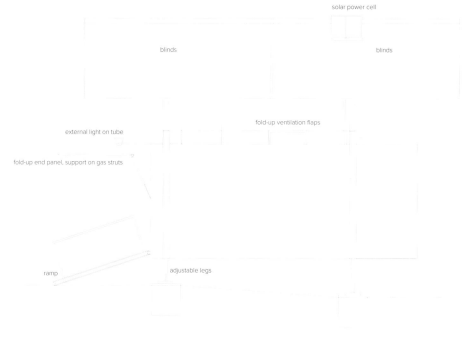

solar power cell

blinds

blinds

fold-up ventilation flaps

external light on tube

fold-up end panel, support on gas struts

ramp

adjustable legs

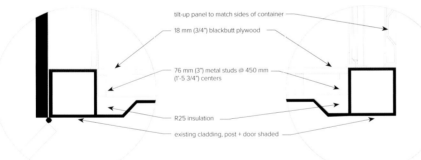

tilt-up panel to match sides of container

18 mm (3/4") blackbutt plywood

76 mm (3") metal studs @ 450 mm
(1'-5 3/4") centers

R25 insulation

existing cladding, post + door shaded

Above Left Using recycled shipping containers takes advantage of an existing global system of transport; it is simple to stockpile the housing units, which are then moved by truck, train, or ship to their new destination. The house is thus truly recyclable, as all the components can be stowed in the container and transported anywhere elsewhere for reuse.

Left The shipping container is transformed into a habitable environment through modifications to the building envelope: R25 thermal insulation is added to the container walls, which are finished on the interior with plywood; operable vents allow for the circulation of fresh air within.

Single Speed Design, Big Dig House, Lexington, Massachusetts, United States

The owner of the home is a civil engineer who was involved with the Big Dig in Boston, a major public works engineering project that dismantled miles of an elevated expressway for a long-awaited underground artery. The engineer commissioned the architects to make use of some of the enormous amounts of construction waste generated, and over 600,000 pounds (272,155.4 kilograms) of the free materials were incorporated into the home as structural components. Cross bracing on the end of the structural frame is left exposed to articulate the separation of load-bearing and enclosure elements. The double-height great room is on the left, with the living and sleeping spaces stacked within the frame.

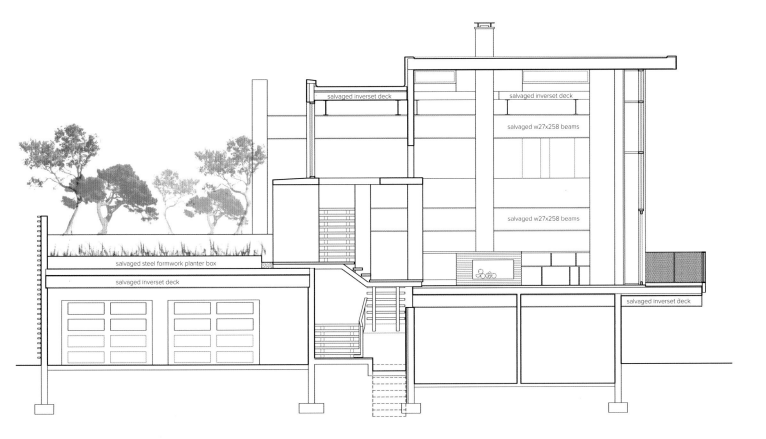

salvaged inverset deck

salvaged inverset deck

salvaged w27x258 beams

salvaged w27x258 beams

salvaged steel formwork planter box

salvaged inverset deck

salvaged inverset deck

Above The design reused steel columns and beams for the frame, concrete and steel inverset decks (concrete roadway) for the floors and roofs, and steel formwork for planters on the roof. The heavy frame easily supports two roof gardens with trees and shrubs over the garage and house that are accessed by an external stair. Concrete masonry unit walls at the garage provide the support for the concrete deck that forms the roof.

Above Right and Right A simple four-column frame brought to the building site in pieces was assembled by crane, using bolted and welded connections. Columns were attached to prepared concrete pier foundations. Since the components were partially prefabricated, the framing was completed in fewer than two days.

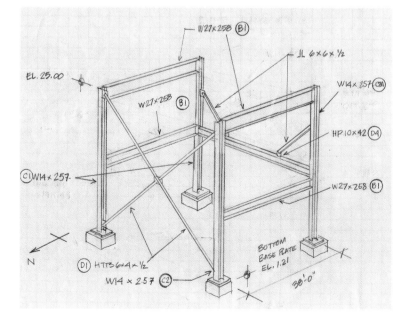

Above As the steel-framed structure is independent of the building envelope, fenestration and partitions could be placed anywhere according to function and composition. The exterior walls are finished with horizontal cedar tongue-and-groove siding. With the frame spanning 38 feet (11.6 meters) in the short direction, most of the ground-floor space remains quite open.

Above Right and Opposite The concrete surfaces and structure of the inverset decks are left exposed on both floor and ceiling. A light-framed steel stair with wood risers connects the two-level house within the heavy steel frame to the great room, adjacent to the frame. Although the steel beams are quite substantial, the lightness and refinement of the architectural detailing maintains a human scale and prevents the structure from being overwhelming.

Directory of Architects and Designers

*Page numbers in parentheses

Architectuurstudio Herman Hertzberger
Gerard Doustraat 220
1073 XB Amsterdam
Netherlands
T 31.20.676.58.88
F 31.20.673.55.10
E office@hertzberger.nl
www.hertzberger.nl

Water Villa, 2002 (62–65, 136–39)*
156 square meters (1,679.2 square feet)

Architekturbüro Rolf Disch
Merzhauser Strasse 177
79100 Freiburg
Germany
T 49.761.459.44.0
F 49.761.459.44.44
E info@rolfdisch.de
www.rolfdisch.de

Solarsiedlung at Schlierberg, 2006 (118–21)
58 row houses and a mixed-use building
on 1 hectare (2.5 acres)

Arkin-Tilt Architects
David Arkin and Anni Tilt
1101 8th Street, 180
Berkeley, CA 94710
United States
T 510.528.9830
F 510.528.0206
E info@arkintilt.com
www.arkintilt.com

Eastern Sierra Residence, 2004 (103–5, 170–71)
3,445 square feet (320.1 square meters)

Atelier Feichang Jianzhu
Yung Ho Chang
Yuan Ming Yuan East Gate
Nei Yard No. 1
Yuan Ming Yuan East Road
100084 Haidian District, Beijing
China

T 86.10.82.62.61.23
F 86.10.82.62.27.12
E fcjz@fcjz.com
www.fcjz.com

Split House, 2002 (66–69)
449 square meters (4,833 square feet)

Balmori Associates
Diana Balmori
820 Greenwich Street, 3rd floor
New York, NY 10014
United States
T 212.431.9191
F 212.431.8616
E info@balmori.com
www.balmori.com

Green Roofs at the Solaire Building, 2003
(96–99) 9,530 square feet (885.4 square meters),
area of roofs

Shigeru Ban Architects
5-2-4 Matsubara
Setagaya, Tokyo
Japan
T 81.3.3324.6760
F 81.3.3324.6789
E Tokyo@ShigeruBanArchitects.com
www.shigerubanarchitects.com

Bamboo Furniture House, 2002 (143–45)
276 square meters (2,970.8 square feet)

Battersby Howat Architects
David Battersby and Heather Howat
1441 East Pender Street
Vancouver, British Columbia V5L 1V7
Canada
T 604.669.9647
F 604.669.2010
general@battersbyhowat.com
www.battersbyhowat.com

Gulf Island Residence, 2004 (46–47, 84–87)
2,500 square feet (232.26 square meters)

Bercy Chen Studio
Thomas Bercy and Calvin Chen
1314 Rosewood Avenue, suite 101
Austin, TX, 78702
United States
T 512.481.0092
E info@bcarc.com
www.bcarc.com

Residence on Annie Street, 2003 (158–59)
2,100 square feet (195.1 square meters)

Residence on Beverly Skyline, 2006 (130–33,
172–73) 2,800 square feet (260.1 square meters)

Breathe Architects
Martin Liefhebber
177 First Avenue
Toronto, Ontario M4M 1X3
Canada
T 416.469.0018
F 416.469.0987
E info@breathebyassociation.com
www.breathebyassociation.com

Port Perry House, 2004 (110–13)
1,700 square feet (157.9 square meters)

Coates Design, with Tim Meldrum
Matthew Coates
P.O. Box 11654
Bainbridge Island, WA 98110
United States
T 206.780.0876
E hello@coatesdesign.com
www.coatesdesign.com

C2C Home, expected 2007/08 (123–27)
2,100 square feet (195.1 square meters)

Cutler Anderson Architects
James Cutler and Bruce Anderson
135 Parfitt Way S.W.
Bainbridge Island, WA 98110
United States
T 206.842.4710
F 206.842.4420
E contact@cutler-anderson.com
www.cutler-anderson.com

Reeve Residence, 2002 (22–25)
2,800 square feet (260.1 square meters)

Bill Dunster Architects
24 Helios Road
Wallington, Surrey SM6 7BZ
United Kingdom
T 44.20.8404.1380
F 44.20.8404.2255
E info@zedfactory.com
www.zedfactory.com

BedZED, 2001 (114–17)
63 homes with workspaces and services
on .64 hectares (1.6 acres)

Matt Gagnon Studio
1013 Grand Street, suite 20
Brooklyn, NY 11211
United States
T 718.384.7724
F 718.384.6473
E info@mattstudio.com
www.mattstudio.com

Driggs Avenue Loft Renovation, 2005 (167–69)
1,500 square feet (139.4 square meters)

Sean Godsell Architects
Level 1 Flinders Lane
Melbourne, Victoria 3000
Australia
T 61.3.9654.2677
F 61.3.9654.3877
E godsell@netspace.net.au
www.seangodsell.com

Future Shack, 2001 (178–79)
15 square meters (161.5 square feet)

Grose Bradley Architects
James Grose and Nicola Bradley
P.O. Box N646
Grosvenor Place, New South Wales 1220
Australia
T 61.2.8297.7200
F 61.2.8297.7299
E mail@grosebradley.com
www.grosebradley.com

Kropach/Catlow Farmhouse, 2003 (37–39,
70–75) 150 square meters (1,614.6 square feet)

David Hertz Architects
2908 Colorado Avenue
Santa Monica, CA 90403
United States
T 310.829.9932
F 310.829.5641
E hertzaia@syndesisinc.com
www.syndesisinc.com

McKinley Residence Addition, 2003 (134–35,
164–65) 2,000 square feet (185.8 square meters)

Steven Holl Architects
450 West 31st Street, 11th floor
New York, NY 10001
United States
T 212.629.7262
F 212.629.7312
E mail@stevenholl.com
www.stevenholl.com

Turbulence House, 2005 (160–63)
900 square feet (83.6 square meters)

Little Tesseract House, 2001 (77–81)
1,250 square feet (116.1 square meters)

Jestico + Whiles
Tom Jestico and John Whiles
1 Cobourg Street
London NW1 2HP
United Kingdom
T 44.20.7380.0382
F 44.20.7380.0511
E jw@jesticowhiles.com
www.jesticowhiles.com

A House for the Future, 2000 (88–89, 128–29)
165 square meters (1,776 square feet)

Jesse Judd Architects
21 Gardiner Street
North Melbourne, Victoria 3051
Australia
T 61.3.9348.9923
F 61.3.9348.9923
E jessejudd@aapt.net.au
www.jessejudd.com.au

Wheatsheaf Residence, 2004 (48–51)
170 square meters (1,829.9 square feet)

Kengo Kuma & Associates
2-24-8 2F Minamiaoyama
Minato-ku, Tokyo 107-0062
Japan
T 81.3.3401.7721
F 81.3.3401.7673
E kuma@ba2.so~net.ne.jp
www.kkaa.co.jp

Great (Bamboo) Wall, 2002 (146–49)
528.6 square meters (5,689.8 square feet)

Michaelis Boyd Associates
Alex Michaelis and Tim Boyd
9B Ladbroke Grove
London W11 3BD
United Kingdom
T 44.297.221.1237
F 44.207.221.0130
E info@michaelisboyd.com
www.michaelisboyd.com

Oxford Gardens Residence, 2004 (52–55)
3,000 square feet (278.7 square meters)

Mole Architects
Meredith Bowles
The Black House, Kingdon Avenue
Prickwillow, Cambridgeshire CB7 4UL
United Kingdom
T 44.1353.688.287
E studio@molearchitects.co.uk
www.molearchitects.co.uk

Black House, 2003 (59–61)
150 square meters (1,614.6 square feet)

Pill Maharam Architects
David Pill
201 Ridge Street
Winchester, MA 01890
United States
T 781.721.7604
F 781.721.5460
www.pillmaharam.com

Great Bay Residence, 2003 (82–83)
3,200 square feet (297.3 square meters)

Travis Price Architects
1111 34th Street NW
Washington, DC 20007
United States
T 202.965.7000
F 202.965.6161
www.travispricearchitects.com

Price Residence, 2004 (42–45)
3,300 square feet (306.6 square meters)

Slavin-Arnholz Residence, 2005 (32–35,
154–57) 2,500 square feet (232.3 square
meters), addition

Pugh + Scarpa Architecture
Angela Brooks and Lawrence Scarpa
2525 Michigan Avenue, Building F1
Santa Monica, CA 90404
United States
T 310.828.0226
F 310.453.9606
E info@pugh-scarpa.com
www.pugh-scarpa.com

Solar Umbrella Residence, 2005 (106–9)
1,900 square feet (176.5 square meters)

Rural Studio
College of Architecture, Design
and Construction
School of Architecture
202 Dudley Commons
Auburn University, AL 36849
United States
T 334.844.5426
F 334.844.5458
E rstudio@auburn.edu
www.ruralstudio.com

Lucy's House, 2002 (174–77)
1,200 square feet (111.5 square meters)

Sambuichi Architects
Hiroshi Sambuichi
8-3-302 Nakajima-cho
Naka-ku, Hiroshima
Japan
T 81.82.544.1417
F 81.82.544.1418
E samb@d2.dion.ne.jp

Sloping North House, 2002 (26–31)
136.5 square meters (1,469.3 square feet)

Stone House, 2005 (90–95)
271.1 square meters (2,918.1 square feet)

Saunders Architecture
Todd Saunders
Vestre torggate 22
NO-5015 Bergen
Norway
T 47.55.36.85.06
F 47.97.52.57.61
E post@saunders.no
www.saunders.no

Summer House, 2002 (40–41)
42 square meters (452.1 square feet)

Shim Sutcliffe Architects
Brigitte Shim and Howard Sutcliffe
441 Queen Street East
Toronto, Ontario M5A 1T5
Canada
T 416.368.3892
F 416.368.9468
E info@shimsut.com
www.shimsutcliffe.com

Island House, 2000 (17–21)
2,000 square feet (185.8 square meters)

Single Speed Design
John Hong and Jinhee Park
171 Brookline Street
Cambridge, MA 02139
United States
T 617.576.9300
F 617.576.7200
E info@singlespeeddesign.com
www.singlespeeddesign.com

Big Dig House, 2005 (180–85)
3,300 square feet (306.6 square meters)

Sivilarkitekt MNAL Tommie Wilhelmsen
Pedersgaten 32
4013 Stavanger
Norway
T 47.917.444.76
E tommie@online.no
www.tommie-wilhelmsen.no

Summer House, 2002 (40–41)
42 square meters (452.1 square feet)

Sarah Wigglesworth Architects
Sarah Wigglesworth and Jeremy Till
9/10 Stock Orchard Street
London N7 9RW
United Kingdom
T 44.20.7607.9200
F 44.20.7607.5800
E email@swarch.co.uk
www.swarch.co.uk

Straw House, 2004 (150–53)
264 square meters (2,841.7 square feet),
residence

Photographer Credits

Tom Arban
Pages 46, 47, 84–87

Arkin-Tilt Architects
Page 171

Satoshi Asakawa, Zoom
Pages 143–49

Balmori Associates
Pages 96, 97, 99

Geoff Barrenger
Pages 110, 112

Peter Bennetts
Pages 6, 48–51

Breathe Architects
Pages 111, 113

Edward Caldwell
Pages 103–5, 170, 171

Earl Carter
Pages 8, 178, 179

Jay Cashman, Inc.
Page 182

Bilyana Dimitrova
Pages 77–81

Georg Nemec, Solarsiedlung
Pages 11, 120, 121

Herman van Doorn
Page 65

James Dow
Pages 10, 17–21

Fawn Art Photography
Page 164

Matt Gagnon Studio
Pages 167–69

Art Grice
Pages 22–25

David Hertz Associates
Pages 134, 135, 165

Architectuurstudio Herman Hertzberger
Pages 62, 64, 136, 139

Steven Holl Architects
Page 162

Timothy Hursley
Pages 174–77

Peter Hyatt
Pages 37, 38, 72–75

The Japan Architect Co.
Pages 26, 27, 29, 30, 90, 91, 93, 94

Ray Main, Mainstream Images
Pages 52–55, 60, 61, 114–17

Ryan Michael, Bercy Chen Studio
Pages 130, 133, 172, 173

Mole Architects
Page 59

Museum of Welsh Life
Pages 88, 128, 129

Mike Osborne
Pages 5, 158, 159

Pill Maharam Architects
Pages 82, 83

Joseph Pettyjohn
Page 131

Marvin Rand
Pages 106, 107, 109

Todd Saunders and Tommie Wilhelmsen
Pages 40, 41

Single Speed Image
Pages 180, 183–85, 191

Paul Smoothy
Pages 150–53

Solarsiedliung
Pages 118, 119

Tim Street-Porter
Page 165

Paul Warchol
Pages 160, 161, 163

Charlotte Wood, Arcblue
Page 89

Kenneth Wyner
Pages 32–35, 42, 43, 45, 154–57

Fu Xing
Pages 66–71

Acknowledgments

I am indebted to my editor, Alicia Kennedy; also to Chris Grimley, our designer, and to Betsy Gammons and the folks at Rockport Publishers for their teamwork on this project. My sincere thanks go to not only all of the designers and photographers for the contribution of inspirational works to this book, but also to their colleagues at each office who addressed my many inquiries. Many thanks as well to Jeff Stein and Karen Bushey for enlightening conversations on current developments in ecological design and energy efficiency. Finally, I am appreciative of my friends and family for their continued encouragement.

Single Speed Design, Big Dig House

About the Author

Yenna Chan has taught design and architectural history and practiced residential architecture in the Boston area. In the past she worked for the architectural journal *Assemblage.* She is now studying toward a Ph.D. in the history of landscape architecture at the Bard Graduate Center in New York.